My Computer

Hardware

Microprocessor: _____

Memory: _____ Megabytes

Hard Drive controller: IDE   SCSI   Local bus (VESA, PCI, etc.)

Hard Drive: Capacity: _____ M   Speed: _____ ms
Other (built-in or "integrated")

Floppy drive 1: 3½-inch   720K   1.4M   2.8M   Other
5¼-inch   1.2M   Other

Floppy drive 2: None
3½-inch   720K   1.4M   2.8M   Other
5¼-inch   1.2M   Other

Graphics standard: VGA   SVGA   8514/a   XGA
Other: _____

Graphics accelerator: NO   YES: _____

Monitor: Diagonal size: _____ inches
Dot pitch: _____ mm
Interlaced   Non-Interlaced
Frequency: _____ MHz   ADJUSTABLE
Type: _____

Keyboard: 101 key "Enhanced"
Other: _____

Printer port(s): LPT1   LPT2   LPT3

Serial port(s): COM1   COM2   COM3   COM4

Joystick port: YES   NO   On sound card

Mouse: Traditional   Trackball   Funky
Serial   Bus
Other info: _____

Busses: ISA   EISA   MCA
PCI   VL (VESA)

IDG BOOKS

Continued on next page →

MY COMPUTER WORKSHEET-HARDWARE

Hardware Goodie — Details

Printer: Dot Matrix: 24-pin 9-pin
CPS: _____ Width: _____
Brand: _____
Laser: PPM: _____
Brand: _____
Remember the printer cable!

Modem: Internal External
Speed: _____ BPS
Hayes compatible? YES NO
Faxing ability? YES NO

Multimedia: Multimedia kit? YES NO
Sound card:
Compatibility: _____
8-bit   16-bit
Joystick port? YES NO
CD-ROM (SCSI) port? YES NO
CD-ROM drive:
Speed: _____ X
Access Time: _____ ms
Internal External
SCSI port? YES NO

Tape Backup: Internal External
Other info: _____

UPS: YES NO

Other: _____
Other: _____
Other: _____

Copyright © 1995
Dan Gookin
All rights reseved
Worksheet $2.95 value.
Item number 485-9

IDG BOOKS

For more information
about IDG Books, call
1-800-762-2947 or 415-655-3000

My Computer Worksheet-Software

Software Category: *Word Processing*
Brand Name: *Doodle Writer*
Developer: *Dood Corp.*
Suggested Retail Price: $*495*
Operating System(s): (DOS) WINDOWS MAC Other: ____
Memory needed: *4* MB
Hard drive space: *8* MB
Graphics: None (VGA) SVGA XGA Other: ____
Sound: None (SoundBlaster) AdLib Other: ____
Printers supported: HP IBM Epson Others: *All Printers!*
Other peripherals: _____
Other peripherals: _____
Type of support: Vanilla - Pay for phone call and support
Chocolate - Pay only for phone call
(Fudge) Free call (800 number)
and free support

SAMPLE

Software Category: _____
Brand Name: _____
Developer: _____
Suggested Retail Price: $____
Operating System(s): DOS WINDOWS MAC Other: ____
Memory needed: ____ MB
Hard drive space: ____ MB
Graphics: None VGA SVGA XGA Other: ____
Sound: None SoundBlaster AdLib Other: ____
Printers supported: HP IBM Epson Others: _____
Other peripherals: _____
Other peripherals: _____
Type of support: Vanilla - Pay for phone call and support
Chocolate - Pay only for phone call
Fudge - Free call (800 number)
and free support

Continued on next page →

IDG BOOKS

My Computer Worksheet-Software

Software Category: _____

Brand Name: _____

Developer: _____

Suggested Retail Price: $_____

Operating System(s): DOS WINDOWS MAC Other: _____

Memory needed: _____ MB

Hard drive space: _____ MB

Graphics: None VGA SVGA XGA Other: _____

Sound: None SoundBlaster AdLib Other: _____

Printers supported: HP IBM Epson Others: _____

Other peripherals: _____

Other peripherals: _____

Type of support: Vanilla - Pay for phone call and support
Chocolate - Pay only for phone call
Fudge - Free call (800 number)
   and free support

Software Category: _____

Brand Name: _____

Developer: _____

Suggested Retail Price: $_____

Operating System(s): DOS WINDOWS MAC Other: _____

Memory needed: _____ MB

Hard drive space: _____ MB

Graphics: None VGA SVGA XGA Other: _____

Sound: None SoundBlaster AdLib Other: _____

Printers supported: HP IBM Epson Others: _____

Other peripherals: _____

Other peripherals: _____

Type of support: Vanilla - Pay for phone call and support
Chocolate - Pay only for phone call
Fudge - Free call (800 number)
   and free support

IDG BOOKS

Copyright © 1995
Dan Gookin
All rights reseved
Worksheet $2.95 value.
Item number 485-9
For more information about IDG Books, call
1-800-762-2947 or 415-655-3000

Buy That Computer!
1995 Edition

by Dan Gookin

IDG BOOKS

IDG Books Worldwide, Inc.
An International Data Group Company

Foster City, CA ♦ Chicago, IL ♦ Indianapolis, IN ♦ Braintree, MA ♦ Dallas, TX

Buy That Computer! 1995 Edition

Published by
IDG Books Worldwide, Inc.
An International Data Group Company
919 E. Hillsdale Blvd.
Suite 400
Foster City, CA 94404

Text and art copyright © 1995 by Dan Gookin. All rights reserved. No part of this book, including interior design, cover design, and icons, may be reproduced or transmitted in any form, by any means (electronic, photocopying, recording, or otherwise) without the prior written permission of the publisher.

Library of Congress Catalog Card No.: 95-75378

ISBN: 1-56884-485-9

Printed in the United States of America

10 9 8 7 6 5 4 3 2 1

1D/QW/QU/ZV

Distributed in the United States by IDG Books Worldwide, Inc.

Distributed by Macmillan Canada for Canada; by Computer and Technical Books for the Caribbean Basin; by Contemporanea de Ediciones for Venezuela; by Distribuidora Cuspide for Argentina; by CITEC for Brazil; by Ediciones ZETA S.C.R. Ltda. for Peru; by Editorial Limusa SA for Mexico; by Transworld Publishers Limited in the United Kingdom and Europe; by Al-Maiman Publishers & Distributors for Saudi Arabia; by Simron Pty. Ltd. for South Africa; by IDG Communications (HK) Ltd. for Hong Kong; by Toppan Company Ltd. for Japan; by Addison Wesley Publishing Company for Korea; by Longman Singapore Publishers Ltd. for Singapore, Malaysia, Thailand, and Indonesia; by Unalis Corporation for Taiwan; by WS Computer Publishing Company, Inc. for the Philippines; by WoodsLane Pty. Ltd. for Australia; by WoodsLane Enterprises Ltd. for New Zealand.

For general information on IDG Books in the U.S., including information on discounts and premiums, contact IDG Books at 800-434-3422 or 415-655-3000.

For information on where to purchase IDG Books outside the U.S., contact IDG Books International at 415-655-3021 or fax 415-655-3295.

For information on translations, contact Marc Jeffrey Mikulich, Director, Foreign & Subsidiary Rights, at IDG Books Worldwide, 415-655-3018 or fax 415-655-3295.

For sales inquiries and special prices for bulk quantities, write to the address above or call IDG Books Worldwide at 415-655-3000.

For information on using IDG Books in the classroom, or ordering examination copies, contact Jim Kelly at 800-434-2086.

For authorization to photocopy items for corporate, personal, or educational use, please contact Copyright Clearance Center, 222 Rosewood Drive, Danvers, MA 01923, or fax 508-750-4470.

Limit of Liability/Disclaimer of Warranty: The author and publisher have used their best efforts in preparing this book. IDG Books Worldwide, Inc., International Data Group, Inc., and the author make no representation or warranties with respect to the accuracy or completeness of the contents of this book and specifically disclaim any implied warranties of merchantability or fitness for any particular purpose and shall in no event be liable for any loss of profit or any other commercial damage, including but not limited to special, incidental, consequential, or other damages.

Trademarks: All brand names and product names used in this book are trademarks, registered trademarks, or trade names of their respective holders. IDG Books Worldwide is not associated with any product or vendor mentioned in this book.

IDG BOOKS is a registered trademark under exclusive license to IDG Books Worldwide, Inc., from International Data Group, Inc.

About the Author

Dan Gookin

Dan Gookin got started with computers back in the post-slide-rule age of computing: 1982. His big break came in 1984, when he began writing about computers. Applying his flair for fiction with a self-taught knowledge of computers, Gookin was able to demystify the subject and explain technology in a relaxed and understandable voice. He even dared to add humor, which eventually won him a column in a local computer magazine.

Eventually, Gookin's talents came to roost as a ghost writer at a computer book publishing house. That was followed by an editing position at a San Diego computer magazine. During this time, he also regularly participated on a radio talk show about computers. In addition, Gookin kept writing books about computers, some of which became minor best-sellers.

In 1990, Gookin came to IDG Books with a book proposal. From that initial meeting unfolded an idea for an outrageous book: a long-overdue and original idea for the computer book for the rest of us. What became *DOS For Dummies* blossomed into an international best-seller with hundreds of thousands of copies in print and many translations.

Today, Gookin still considers himself a writer and computer "guru" whose job it is to remind everyone that computers are not to be taken too seriously. He knows that the complex beasts are important and can help people become productive and successful. Gookin mixes his knowledge of computers with a unique, dry sense of humor that keeps everyone informed — and awake. His favorite quote is "Computers are a notoriously dull subject, but that doesn't mean I have to write about them that way."

Gookin's titles for IDG Books include the best-selling *DOS For Dummies* and *WordPerfect For Dummies*, *WordPerfect 6 For Dummies*, *PCs For Dummies*, *Word For Windows For Dummies*, and the *Illustrated Computer Dictionary For Dummies*. Gookin holds a degree in communications from the University of California-San Diego and currently lives with his wife and boys in the as-yet-untamed state of Idaho.

Dedication

This book is dedicated to all first-time computer shoppers and just about anyone who's felt frustration when buying a computer.

Acknowledgments

I'd like to thank Jack Dunning, Tina Rathbone, and Al Telles for their contributions to this book's first incarnation, oh, maybe eight years ago. For this version I'd like to thank Chris Wagner, Jerry Hewett, and Ken Jacobsen. I forgot what they did, but I shall thank them anyway.

Thanks to Matt Wagner at Waterside for finding a home for this book after it sat around ignored for five years. Thanks to John Kilcullen and David Solomon at IDG Books for *eventually* picking up this book as a new series. (Others at IDG are listed on the Credits page.)

The publisher and I would both like to acknowledge and thank Patrick McGovern, the genius behind IDG, without whom none of this would have been possible.

ABOUT IDG BOOKS WORLDWIDE

Welcome to the world of IDG Books Worldwide.

IDG Books Worldwide, Inc., is a subsidiary of International Data Group, the world's largest publisher of computer-related information and the leading global provider of information services on information technology. IDG was founded more than 25 years ago and now employs more than 7,200 people worldwide. IDG publishes more than 233 computer publications in 65 countries (see listing below). More than sixty million people read one or more IDG publications each month.

Launched in 1990, IDG Books Worldwide is today the #1 publisher of best-selling computer books in the United States. We are proud to have received 3 awards from the Computer Press Association in recognition of editorial excellence, and our best-selling ...For Dummies™ series has more than 12 million copies in print with translations in 25 languages. IDG Books, through a recent joint venture with IDG's Hi-Tech Beijing, became the first U.S. publisher to publish a computer book in the People's Republic of China. In record time, IDG Books has become the first choice for millions of readers around the world who want to learn how to better manage their businesses.

Our mission is simple: Every IDG book is designed to bring extra value and skill-building instructions to the reader. Our books are written by experts who understand and care about our readers. The knowledge base of our editorial staff comes from years of experience in publishing, education, and journalism — experience which we use to produce books for the '90s. In short, we care about books, so we attract the best people. We devote special attention to details such as audience, interior design, use of icons, and illustrations. And because we use an efficient process of authoring, editing, and desktop publishing our books electronically, we can spend more time ensuring superior content and spend less time on the technicalities of making books.

You can count on our commitment to deliver high-quality books at competitive prices on topics consumers want to read about. At IDG, we value quality, and we have been delivering quality for more than 25 years. You'll find no better book on a subject than an IDG book.

John Kilcullen
President and CEO
IDG Books Worldwide, Inc.

VIII WINNER — Eighth Annual Computer Press Awards ≥ 1992

IX WINNER — Ninth Annual Computer Press Awards ≥ 1993

IDG Books Worldwide, Inc., is a subsidiary of International Data Group, the world's largest publisher of computer-related information and the leading global provider of information services on information technology. International Data Group publishes over 220 computer publications in 65 countries. More than fifty million people read one or more International Data Group publications each month. The officers are Patrick J. McGovern, Founder and Board Chairman; Kelly Conlin, President; Jim Casella, Chief Operating Officer. International Data Group's publications include: **ARGENTINA'S** Computerworld Argentina, Infoworld Argentina; **AUSTRALIA'S** Computerworld Australia, Computer Living, Australian PC World, Australian Macworld, Network World, Mobile Business Australia, Publish!, Reseller, IDG Sources; **AUSTRIA'S** Computerwelt Oesterreich, PC Test; **BELGIUM'S** Data News (CW); **BOLIVIA'S** Computerworld; **BRAZIL'S** Computerworld, Connections, Game Power, Mundo Unix, PC World, Publish, Super Game; **BULGARIA'S** Computerworld Bulgaria, PC & Mac World Bulgaria, Network World Bulgaria; **CANADA'S** CIO Canada, Computerworld Canada, InfoCanada, Network World Canada, Reseller; **CHILE'S** Computerworld Chile, Informatica; **COLOMBIA'S** Computerworld Colombia, PC World; **COSTA RICA'S** PC World; **CZECH REPUBLIC'S** Computerworld, Elektronika, PC World; **DENMARK'S** Communications World, Computerworld Danmark, Computerworld Focus, Macintosh Produktkatalog, Macworld Danmark, PC World Danmark, PC Produktguide, Tech World, Windows World; **ECUADOR'S** PC World Ecuador; **EGYPT'S** Computerworld (CW) Middle East, PC World Middle East; **FINLAND'S** MikroPC, Tietoviikko, Tietoverkko; **FRANCE'S** Distributique, GOLDEN MAC, InfoPC, Le Guide du Monde Informatique, Le Monde Informatique, Telecoms & Reseaux; **GERMANY'S** Computerwoche, Computerwoche Focus, Computerwoche Extra, Electronic Entertainment, Gamepro, Information Management, Macwelt, Netzwelt, PC Welt, Publish, Publish& Multimedia World; **GREECE'S** Publish & Macworld; **HONG KONG'S** Computerworld Hong Kong, PC World Hong Kong; **HUNGARY'S** Computerworld SZT, PC World; **INDIA'S** Computers & Communications; **INDONESIA'S** Info Komputer; **IRELAND'S** ComputerScope; **ISRAEL'S** Beyond Windows, Computerworld Israel, Multimedia, PC World Israel; **ITALY'S** Computerworld Italia, Lotus Magazine, Macworld Italia, Networking Italia, PC Shopping Italy, PC World Italia; **JAPAN'S** Computerworld Today, Information Systems World, Macworld Japan, Nikkei Personal Computing, SunWorld Japan, Windows World; **KENYA'S** East African Computer News; **KOREA'S** Computerworld Korea, Macworld Korea, PC World Korea; **LATIN AMERICA'S** GamePro; **MALAYSIA'S** Computerworld Malaysia, PC World Malaysia; **MEXICO'S** Compu Edicion, Compu Manufactura, Computacion/Punto de Venta, Computerworld Mexico, MacWorld, Mundo Unix, PC World, Windows; **THE NETHERLANDS'** Computer! Totaal, Computable (CW), LAN Magazine, Lotus Magazine, MacWorld; **NEW ZEALAND'S** Computer Buyer, Computerworld New Zealand, Network World, New Zealand PC World; **NIGERIA'S** PC World Africa; **NORWAY'S** Computerworld Norge, Lotusworld Norge, Macworld Norge, Maxi Data, Networld, PC World Ekspress, PC World Nettverk, PC World Norge, PC World's Produktguide, Publish&r Multimedia World, Student Data, Unix World, Windowsworld; **PAKISTAN'S** PC World Pakistan; **PANAMA'S** PC World Panama; **PERU'S** Computerworld Peru, PC World; **PEOPLE'S REPUBLIC OF CHINA'S** China Computerworld, China Infoworld, China PC Info Magazine, Computer Fan, PC World China, Electronics International, Electronics Today/Multimedia World, Electronic Product World, China Network World, Software World Magazine, Telecom Product World; **PHILIPPINES'** Computerworld Philippines, PC Digest (PCW); **POLAND'S** Computerworld Poland, Computerworld Special Report, Networld, PC World/Komputer, Sunworld; **PORTUGAL'S** CerebroyPC World, Correio Informatico/Computerworld, MacIn; **ROMANIA'S** Computerworld, PC World, Telecom Romania; **RUSSIA'S** Computerworld-Moscow, Mir - PK (PCW), Sety (Networks); **SINGAPORE'S** Computerworld Southeast Asia, PC World Singapore; **SLOVENIA'S** Monitor Magazine; **SOUTH AFRICA'S** Computer Mail (CIO),Computing S.A.,Network World S.A., Software World; **SPAIN'S** Advanced Systems, Amiga World, Computerworld Espana, Communicaciones World, Macworld Espana, NeXTWORLD, Super Juegos Magazine (GamePro), PC World Espana, Publish; **SWEDEN'S** Attack, ComputerSweden, Corporate Computing, Macworld, Mikrodatorn, Natverk &r Kommunikation, PC World, CAP & Design, Datalngenjoren, Maxi Data,Windows World; **SWITZERLAND'S** Computerworld Schweiz, Macworld Schweiz, PC Tip; **TAIWAN'S** Computerworld Taiwan, PC World Taiwan; **THAILAND'S** Thai Computerworld; **TURKEY'S** Computerworld Monitor, Macworld Turkiye, PC World Turkiye; **UKRAINE'S** Computerworld, Computers+Software Magazine; **UNITED KINGDOM'S** Computing /Computerworld, Connexion/Network World, Lotus Magazine, Macworld, Open Computing/Sunworld; **UNITED STATES'** Advanced Systems, AmigaWorld, Cable in the Classroom, CD Review, CIO, Computerworld, Computerworld Client/Server Journal, Digital Video, DOS World, Electronic Entertainment Magazine (E2), Federal Computer Week, Game Hits, GamePro, IDG Books, Infoworld, Laser Event, Macworld, Maximize, Multimedia World, Network World, PC Letter, PC World, Publish, SWATPro, Video Event; **URUGUAY'S** PC World Uruguay; **VENEZUELA'S** Computerworld Venezuela, PC World; **VIETNAM'S** PC World Vietnam.

03/01/95

Credits

Executive Vice President, Strategic Product Planning and Research
David Solomon

SVP & Publisher
Milissa L. Koloski

Editorial Director
Diane Graves Steele

Acquisitions Editor
Megg Bonar

Brand Manager
Judith A. Taylor

Editorial Managers
Sandra Blackthorn
Kristin A. Cocks

Editorial Assistants
Stacey Holden Prince
Kevin Spencer

Acquisitions Assistant
Suki Gear

Production Director
Beth Jenkins

Supervisor of Project Coordination
Cindy L. Phipps

Pre-Press Coordinator
Steve Peake

Associate Pre-Press Coordinator
Tony Augsburger

Project Editor
Kristin A. Cocks

Editors
Mike Kelly
Suzanne Packer

Technical Reviewers
Ron Dippold
Jamey Marcum

Production Staff
Paul Belcastro
Linda M. Boyer
J. Tyler Connor
Carla Radzikinas
Dwight Ramsey
Patricia R. Reynolds
Theresa Sánchez-Baker
Gina Scott

Proofreader
Sandra Profant

Indexer
Sherry Massey

Cover Design
Draper and Liew, Inc.

Contents at a Glance

Foreword xiii
Introduction 1
Chapter 1: How to Buy a Computer 5
Chapter 2: What Can a Computer Do for Me? 13
Chapter 3: Shopping for an Operation System 17
Chapter 4: Shopping for Software 25
Chapter 5: The Software Cavalcade 33
Chapter 6: The Microprocessor 47
Chapter 7: Memory (RAM) 57
Chapter 8: Disk Drives 65
Chapter 9: The Monitor and Keyboard 75
Chapter 10: Ports, Mouses, and Other Stuff 85
Chapter 11: All About Printers 97
Chapter 12: Peripherals 109
Chapter 13: Shopping for Service and Support 121
Chapter 14: Buying Your Computer 129
Chapter 15: About Your Computer System 141
Appendix A: Commonly Asked Questions 147
Appendix B: Where to Find More Information 155
Glossary and Index 159
Reader Response Card .... Back of Book

Table of Contents

Foreword xiii

Introduction 1
    Wait. Do You Really Want to Do This? 1
    The Computer Revolution Myth 1
    About This Book 2
    What Do I Do Now? 3

Chapter 1: How to Buy a Computer 5
    The Five Steps to Buying a Computer 6
    Waiting for the Technology Bus 11
    Quick Review 12

Chapter 2: What Can a Computer Do for Me? 13
    Which Questions to Ask 14
    Your Computer's Potential 15
    Quick Review 16

Chapter 3: Shopping for an Operating System 17
    Understanding Operating Systems 17
    Choosing an Operating System 22
    Quick Review 23

Chapter 4: Shopping for Software 25
    How to Buy Software 25
    Looking at the Software Box 29
    Quick Review 32

Chapter 5: The Software Cavalcade 33

Word Processors 33
Spreadsheets 34
Databases 36
Graphics 37
Communications Software 38
Recreation 39
Education 39
Utilities 39
Programming 40
Multimedia Software 41
Software for Free 42
Bundled Software 44
Integrated Versus Stand-Alone Software 44
Quick Review 46

Chapter 6: The Microprocessor 47

The Microprocessor 48
Quick Review 55

Chapter 7: Memory (RAM) 57

Temporary Storage: Computer Memory (or RAM) 58
Quick Review 64

Chapter 8: Disk Drives 65

The Hard Drive 66
The Floppy Drive 70
Quick Review 73

Chapter 9: The Monitor and Keyboard 75

The Monitor ("Look at Me! I'm as Pretty as a Trinitron TV!") 75

Keyboards 80
Quick Review 83

Chapter 10: Ports, Mouses, and Other Stuff 85

Ports 85
Mouses and Other Non-Furry
"Pointing Devices" 91
Catching the Right Bus 93
Quick Review 96

Chapter 11: All About Printers 97

Yes, There Is a Vast Selection 97
Dot Matrix Printers 100
Ink Jet and Color Printers 103
Thermal Printers 104
Laser Printers 104
The PC Printer Compatibility Issue 106
Quick Review 107

Chapter 12: Peripherals 109

Modems and Faxes 109
Multimedia and Sound 114
Other Peripherals: Optical Disks,
Tape Backup Units, Scanners, and
Backup Power Supplies 116
Quick Review 119

Chapter 13: Shopping for Service and Support 121

Finding Service and Support for Your PC ... 121
The Dealer Service and
Support Worksheet 125
Quick Review 128

Chapter 14: Buying Your Computer ... 129

Putting It All Together 129
Reading a Computer Ad 132
Where to Buy 134
And the Final Step Is To 138
Quick Review 140

Chapter 15: About Your Computer System 141

Setting Up Your PC 141
Breaking It In (The "Burn-In" Test) 145
Learning Your System 146
Quick Review 146

Appendix A: Commonly Asked Questions 147

Software 147
Microprocessors 148
Disk Drives 149
Monitors and Keyboards 149
Printers and Peripherals 150
Computer Systems 152
General 153

Appendix B: Where to Find More Information 155

Computer Magazines 155
Computer Books 156
Computer User Groups 156

Glossary and Index 159

Reader Response Card ..... Back of Book

Foreword

Educating the public about computers is top on my list.

I consider you more important than the technology you're going to read about in this book. Because of that, this book is written in a relaxed, easy-to-read style. I try not to confuse. Computers are notoriously dull and boring, but that doesn't mean that I have to write about them that way. This book maintains an entertaining and informative reading style because computers aren't life-threatening, and no one should write about them that way.

Read this book and you'll soon be an expert, happily being productive with your new computer system. There's no tedium. No techno-jargon. No frantic lunacy. Just plain, enjoyable, and informative English text. So relax already and start reading!

> Dan Gookin
> January, 1995

Introduction

Before things get moving, there are a few, careful points I want to make. Nothing scary, mind you. Just a few facts to confirm, some soothing words of advice, a gentle pat on the back. Then the fireworks start.

Wait. Do You Really Want To Do This?

Before stuffing any new information into your head, you should do three simple things:

Relax. Sit back. Don't panic.

Buying a computer is a scary thing to do. It costs a lot of money. It's a big question mark. There's no sense in telling you the *Big Lie* that computers are easy and simple. They're not. They're powerful tools, yes. But the problem most folks have is that they expect all the answers without any work. If cars were a new concept to society, buying them would be scary as well.

Computers are complex, but they aren't difficult to master. This book helps resolve some of the complexities. It does so without pain or trauma. So, if you have any doubts about going further, continue reading. Those doubts will soon vanish.

The Computer Revolution Myth

A long time ago, there was an advertising campaign about the "Computer Revolution." It was here. It was happening. You would be left in the intellectual dust if you didn't buy a computer — especially for your kids. Society would soon be composed of the haves and the have-nots. You wouldn't be able to get a job. Buying a computer was considered more important than having a use for one.

Poppycock.

The computer revolution never happened. True, revolutionary advances in computers are taking place everyday. But the big revolution? Computers in every den? Bah! It was more a parade than a revolution. The parade is long since over, and most folks are sitting at home wondering what it all meant.

Slowly, the personal computer has evolved from a hobbyist's play-toy to a unique and valuable tool. The computer is a time saver, an electric file cabinet, an organizer, a quick thinker. Although it may not be a solution to any specific problem, the computer allows people to become more productive and perform mundane and repetitive tasks quickly.

The second part of the computer revolution myth involved becoming "computer literate." True, there is such a thing as computer literacy. However, for most people, becoming computer literate doesn't imply that you absolutely must rush out and buy a computer.

Computer literacy implies that you can go to an all-night teller machine, punch the right buttons, and have money appear. That's it. As long as you're able to do the things society requires of you — and those things require using some form of mechanical, computerized device — you're computer literate. Knowing how to program a computer, or take apart and fix one, is not part of computer literacy. Don't let anyone fool you into thinking otherwise.

About This Book

This book is meant to be read from front to back. You won't need a technical dictionary to read this book. And because it never gets any more complicated than this paragraph, you don't need a computer, either.

Each chapter of this book is meant to slowly unravel the mystery of computers. Each computer concept is covered one at a time. Sadly, no one else will bother to do this for you. People — especially salesmen — never bother to explain computer words: what they are, what they mean, and most significantly, whether or not they're important to you.

This book presents you with information and new concepts one item at a time. Occasionally you may cross a term that seems obscure to you. When this happens (hopefully never), that term will appear in *italic* text. Turn to the Glossary for a definition. Otherwise, each chapter breaks down and introduces computer concepts in a (what else?) logical way.

GREAT ADVICE Another thing I couldn't leave out is my own buying advice. This information is flagged in the text with an icon, similar to the one you see floating next to this paragraph. The icon signals that you're reading my recommendations — some good advice on which way to go when there's a decision to be made or some looming doubt.

What Do I Do Now?

Start with Chapter 1 and learn about the five steps to take when buying a computer. The chapters in the rest of the book flow naturally after that. Only when you're done reading are you ready to buy. So put away your wallet — don't sit and fuss over your bank balance just yet. Sit back and relax. It's almost time to buy that computer.

CHAPTER 1
How to Buy a Computer

The Five Steps You Should Follow

Buying a computer is not all that terrible. It doesn't have to be. Sure, there's jargon, a smidgen of fear and doubt, a whiff of uncertainty about advancing technology and being left behind, and the computer itself — one of life's most notorious villains. Yet to be honest, you want to own one and know it's a good thing. I'm happy to tell you that the buying process can be quite easy. Pleasant, in fact.

Buying a computer is like buying anything else: the more you know about what it is you're buying, the easier it is to make the proper decisions. The purpose of this book is to get you oriented and informed so the buying process becomes simple and (what else?) logical. The end result is that you get the computer you want and the support you need without feeling you've been cheated. Very soon you'll find yourself sitting in front of that computer, proudly telling *it* what to do for *you*.

It all starts with the five steps you should take when buying a computer. The steps provide a logical breakdown of the things you should cover — the decisions you need to make — that give you a painless computer-buying experience. The points here will be amplified throughout this book. But for a quick 'n dirty preview, here they are:

> ### Five steps to buying a computer
> 1. Decide what you want the computer to do.
> 2. Find the software that will get you the desired result.
> 3. Find the hardware to run your software.
> 4. Shop for service and support.
> 5. Buy that computer!

The Five Steps to Buying a Computer

There are as many reasons to consider buying a personal computer as there are people to think up the reasons. And there are more benefits to owning a computer than could possibly be listed — even by a computer. But for whatever reason you're considering one, there are a few simple steps you should take before you buy a computer.

Step 1: Decide what you want your computer to do

The biggest crime made when buying a computer is buying one "just because." I once knew a woman who decided she wanted a computer. She had no reason for buying a computer, though after a time "to do word processing" seemed to surface. Yet this person never used a typewriter and had no need to write anything more than a grocery list. For her, buying a computer was a bad decision because she had no use for it. This isn't to say that computers are useless to most people. Quite the contrary; computers can help anyone. (This person had made the mistake of not asking herself a few questions before moving on to step two.)

> ### "Why doesn't everyone own a computer?"
>
> So if computers are just so great, why doesn't everyone have one?
>
> Off the top of your head, you may think of a few reasons: they're too complicated, too expensive, too difficult to master, and so on. Yet surveys have shown that a good 60 percent of people don't own a computer for one simple reason: They can't find any use for them.
>
> The problem is education. Computers can do anything for anyone, but that word hasn't gotten out yet. As soon as more people learn about what a computer can do for them, more people will be interested in buying them.

Once you've decided what it is you want to do with your computer, you should look for computer software. It's the software that does the work. For example, you buy a VCR so you can record TV shows and rent movies; that's the reason you own a VCR, not just because it looks technologically imposing sitting on the TV.

A computer is basically a box of electronics, and this box can be told to do a number of things. Computer programs are instructions for the computer that make it behave in a certain manner. For example, a computer is capable of working both with numbers and words; it's the software that directs the computer to work with either one or the other.

Any computer you might consider buying will have a variety of software available for it. These types of software are discussed in Chapter 6.

Each type of software does a specific thing. Word processing software is the most popular kind of software sold to businesses; games and educational software dominate the home market. Other kinds of software have their own uses, and some software, called *integrated software*, combines several software packages into one program.

Although, categorically, each type of software does a basic job, there are many, many companies making software. This brings up the next step:

Step 2: Find the software that will get you the desired result

Even if you've decided it's yak herding that you most need a computer for, you're in luck; there's probably a computer program out there just for you. Most everyone, from the yak herder to the zither repairperson, will be delighted to find computer software just for them. For most folks, the software you need exists in abundance and is bound to help you do whatever it is you do do.

Suppose that you've decided you'd like a computer to help you with your word processing. Dozens of word processing software packages are available, all catering to the needs of different writers.

Choosing the software you need before choosing a computer can be really tough. After all, you're buying a *computer* (the hardware). It's what you'll spend the most money on and what people will see. You don't see the computer's software, which is more important. Looking at only the software and ignoring the machine can be difficult — especially if someone has biased you against a particular brand or machine before you start shopping.

Eventually, you'll locate the specific software you feel comfortable with, and once you do:

Step 3: Find the hardware that will run the selected software

Software controls hardware. Not only that, software *consumes* hardware. It eats it up, digesting huge amounts of microprocessor horsepower, memory, disk space, graphics, printers, and the whole lot — what's called *hardware* in the computer biz. After you find your software, it's your job to survey computer hardware and assemble a PC that has enough of the proper kind of hardware to meet your software's voracious appetite.

A big mistake people often make when buying a computer is assuming computers are all one and the same. After all, one computer box looks like another. But it's what's inside the box that runs your software, so you'll need to decide how much *memory* to put in your computer, what size of *hard drive* to get, and how fancy you want your graphics. These decisions aren't that difficult, providing you know your software's appetite for graphics, memory, and hard drive space. (This book shows you the ropes in Part III.)

Other computer hardware sits outside the main computer box. These items are called *peripherals,* and the most important of them is the *printer.* If you're using the computer for word processing, the printer is what you'll need to get a *hard copy* of your written words. If you're using a spreadsheet, the printer provides the hard copy needed for the record books.

The leading role of the operating system

Tightly bound into your computer and its software is the *operating system*. It acts as the main program on your computer — the most important piece of software, since it controls the entire computer. The operating system provides the vital link between your computer's hardware and its software. (This subject is covered in detail in Chapter 3.)

Choosing a printer is a big, big decision because there are many kinds and styles of printers. In Chapter 11, you'll learn about which type of printer is best for your own particular use.

"Should I buy a used computer?"

I don't recommend buying a used computer as your first computer purchase. Often these computers are just as capable as new computers, though they may not be as powerful. And they're affordable. But the main drawback is a lack of proper service and support. You can't really expect someone who's unloading an old PC to be like a dedicated computer store that's set up to deal with problems, support, service, and training. Also, used computers have no warranty, which should immediately shut the door on this idea in your mind.

For a second computer purchase, or for buying the kids a computer, a used computer can be a good idea. Please use the same advice offered in this book for buying a used computer as you would a new one. The only difference is that you will already have your software. (So take the software with you and make sure that it runs on the used computer before you buy.)

Before signing on the bottom line, you'll need to do one very important and oft forgotten thing:

Step 4: Find service and support for your hardware and software

Support is a big word in computers and, unfortunately, something many buyers neglect. It means, "We're here to help you after you buy the computer and software." It's possible to buy a computer and software and then sit at home totally stuck. If you have support, then there's someone to call, as well as a place to go, to explain your problem and get help. In the complex world of computers, believe me when I tell you support is a necessity.

Support can be divided into two general categories: training and service.

Training is where a dealer offers classes (usually included with the purchase price), teaching you how to set up, operate, and use your new computer. Occasionally, classes on specific pieces of software are offered.

Service is divided into two parts. The first deals with the repair of the computer should something go wrong. If your computer breaks, you should be able to take it back to where you bought it to get it fixed. It's even better if your computer can be fixed at the store, avoiding any shipping delays.

The second part of service is answering questions. Does the store accept phone calls? Can you come in and expect someone to sit down with you and answer your questions? This is something to be very picky about. Quite a few salespeople will claim that they can't answer questions and will refer you to a technical person. Make sure that those technicians are available (that is, that they're not "out" a lot). This is something you should find out about before you spend any money.

Chapter 1: How to Buy a Computer

> ### How to buy those wee li'l laptop computers?
>
> A special type of computer is the *laptop computer*, which can be just as powerful and capable as the larger, traditional *desktop PC* but can weigh less than six pounds and fit in a lunch box. All the information in this book applies to both laptop and desktop computers.

The final step to take is:

Step 5: Buy that computer!

Go for it!

Once all the pieces are present, fit them together. Go out and buy yourself a personal computer! Being well prepared and having thought through your decision, you should have few worries. As soon as everything is as you want it to be, you and your computer will be spending many happy, productive hours together.

Waiting for the Technology Bus

Before moving on, there's always some hesitation once you're ready to buy your computer. In fact, "Step 5: Buy that computer!" is the hardest of all the steps.

It's not the money that keeps some people from buying a computer. No, it's the rapid advancement of technology. Computer technology zooms ahead quickly. A computer that you buy today is guaranteed to be obsolete in six years, nearly useless in ten. People see this as a warning: Don't buy today's computer; wait for the next generation.

Although it's true that the next generation of computers will be better, faster, and probably less expensive, it's also true that waiting for it gets you nowhere. It's like not catching a bus because you assume the next bus will have fewer people on it or will be cleaner. That may be the case, but while you're waiting, you're not going anywhere.

The bottom line is when you're ready to buy, *buy*.

✔ Quick Review

There are five important steps to buying a computer:

1. Decide what you want the computer to do.
2. Find the software that will get you the desired result.
3. Find the hardware to run your software.
4. Shop for service and support.
5. Buy that computer!

The most important of these steps is the first one: having a purpose in mind for the computer. You don't have to think hard about how a computer can help you. In fact, anyone who uses a calculator or a typewriter has an immediate use for a computer.

Once you find a way that a computer can help you, the rest is just following the steps and becoming well informed. This book will make you well informed. You must follow the steps on your own.

CHAPTER 2
"What Can a Computer Do for Me?"

Asking Yourself Some Important Questions before Buying

The question that a computer buyer most commonly asks is, "Which computer should I buy?" But the computer is just hardware. More important than which computer (or hardware) you buy is the software you plan to use. It's the software that controls the hardware. So the key question here is, "What do you plan on doing with your computer?"

The object of asking yourself questions is to find out how you'll be using the computer. Once you know that, then you find software to do the job and then match hardware to your software. That's the best way to end up happy with a computer.

> **Software and disks**
>
> Software comes on diskettes, but the diskette itself isn't really the software. Instead, the software is magnetically encoded on the surface of the diskette, just like music is recorded on a cassette tape. Unlike computer hardware, which you can touch, feel, and drop on the floor, computer software is the stuff you cannot touch. (You can refer to Chapter 8 for more information on floppy disks.)

Which Questions to Ask

Odds are pretty good that you probably know what you want a computer for. If so, great. Please review the questions in this chapter's summary and move on to Chapter 3. If you don't really know what you want your computer for, keep reading and (trust me) it will come to you.

Thanks to software, computers can do just about anything. Primarily, computers help you do work; doing repetitive tasks is a computer's star quality. After that, they educate and entertain. This means that computers can do just about anything for anyone.

Before you ask yourself the questions, take a good look at your job, your hobbies, and your life. What do you spend time on? What do you dabble with? What would you like to do or explore? Never start by saying, "I have a computer, now what?"

The best question to ask

The first and best question to ask yourself is:

What do I see me doing with a computer?

Notice the question isn't, "What am I doing with this new IBM technological powerhouse?" Instead, the focus here is on your work. What will the computer help you do?

Another worthy question

Often times, the questions you need to ask yourself deal with computers that may already influence your life:

What do I do on other computers that I would want to do on my home computer?

For example, if you already have a computer at the office, what do you do with it? Further, what do you do on the office computer that you would also need a home computer for? (If you're buying a computer for the office and already have one at home, then you really need to go back and restate the first question found in the preceding section: What do I see me doing with a computer at the office?)

If you're buying a computer for your kids, what do they do with it at school? Find out what software they use. Talk with the computer manager or computer science teacher. They'll probably have some wonderful suggestions for you. (But keep in mind you're on the *software* stage now; put off the "this is a great place to shop" pointers for now.)

The "Okay, I'm really stuck" questions

Not everyone is going to be blessed by finding that one software package right there on the shelf, the package that screams, "I'm everything you ever wanted to do on a computer." Sure, it may happen, but most of the time it won't.

When the answers to these questions don't give you the name of a specific type of software program, you need to think more generally about what you do and how a computer can help.

Here are a few questions you should mull over in your head:

What do I spend the most time on?

What activities are the most repetitive?

Do I do anything that involves lists or organizing information?

Do I ever sit with a calculator to work out problems for more than a few minutes?

Do I ever sit with a typewriter for more than a few minutes each week?

Don't let even the smallest excuse steer you away from the computer. No matter what it is you do, a computer can help you do it better, faster, and much more easily. Trust me, software exists to do just about anything. It's up to you to match your needs to that software.

Your Computer's Potential

A computer is capable of just about anything. What makes it so capable is the software that controls the computer. Software's primary duty is to tell the computer what to do, and it can tell the computer to do anything the computer is capable of (and even "fake" some things the computer isn't). This is how a single computer can be used as a word processor, a graphics design workstation, and even an arcade game. It's the different software programs that tell the computer what to do.

Something that you need to do is discover what the computer can do for you. This may be something that's overly obvious to you. For example, I bought my first computer as a replacement for my typewriter. Anyone in any business will find a computer valuable for doing the books, correspondence, design, keeping a customer data-base, and on and on. Even if you don't think a computer can do anything for you, chances are you only need to get up to speed on what computers are capable of today.

A great example I like to cite is genealogy. It's a burning passion with lots of folks. Unfortunately, genealogists kept track of their family roots on 3x5 cards and used color markers to have it all make sense. Enter the computer!

Computers are wonderful tools for tracking information. Specifically in this case, computers are whizzes at the *database* — a collection of records or index cards, similar to the 3x5 cards amateur genealogists kept information about their ancestors on. By using computers, the genealogists found the task of keeping track of their long-gone relatives a snap. This advancement spawned a whole subculture of genealogy nuts using computers.

Like the genealogists, you may discover that the computer has something special to offer you, something you may not be thinking of right now. That process of discovery starts when you ask yourself the questions at the beginning of this chapter.

✔ Quick Review

Before you even start thinking about buying a computer, you need to think about what you'll be doing with it. The task you want to do will be carried out by computer software, and that software is what controls the computer hardware that you'll eventually buy.

Here are a few of the questions you should mull over before you start shopping for computer software:

1. What do you see yourself doing with your computer?
2. How do you spend most of your time?
3. What activities are the most repetitive?
4. Do you do anything that involves lists or organizing information?
5. Do you ever work with a calculator or typewriter for more than a few minutes each week?

Chapter 3
Shopping for an Operating System

Choosing Your Computer's Main Control Program

Without any software to control your computer, you essentially have a very expensive paperweight on your desk. Just go ahead and ask around; you'll find lots of computer owners with various *boat anchors* in their closets or used as doorstops. These were impressive machines, but they lacked the proper software to harness their hardware horsepower.

Fortunately, you won't own a boat anchor computer. You have the foresight to see how much a lack of software can hurt a computer — no matter how impressive the hardware. Software really is the key.

Central to all software in your computer is the main piece of software. It's that one program that controls all the others and just about everything else in your computer. It's the first program run in the morning, the program that other programs defer to, the head program in charge, the boss, the czar, *el queso grande*, the king o' everything. It's called the *operating system*.

Understanding Operating Systems

An operating system is a program that controls your computer; specifically, it controls the main chip in your computer, called the *microprocessor*. Together, the microprocessor and operating system are at the heart of the computer; they go hand in hand.

The microprocessor sits on your computer's throne. You could say it's your computer's "brain," but the microprocessor holds no hideous intelligence and is really only good at carrying out orders. It's the computer's operating system (software) that tells the microprocessor how to control the computer. In fact, if there were a "brain" in the computer, it would be the operating system, not the microprocessor. Without instructions from the operating system, the microprocessor chip might as well be a potato chip (though not as salty).

After controlling the microprocessor, and therefore the rest of the computer's hardware, the operating system has a second job: It controls all the other software on your computer.

For example, suppose that you use a word processor to write the next *Gone With the Wind*. That word processor is software — a computer program. But it must work with your computer's operating system to be completely happy. When you choose software for your new computer, you select it for which operating system it runs on (or is compatible with) more than you select it for a particular computer.

So in the chore of buying a computer, software comes first, but the first software is the computer's operating system. Without the operating system, the hardware and all your software would be useless. (Buying software is covered in Chapter 4.)

Compatibility is the key

Over the past dozen years or so, a lot of computers with a lot of microprocessors and even more operating systems have come and gone. The most successful computers have survived because of *compatibility,* which implies that a computer can run a lot of software. Unless a computer has access to a large *software base,* its success is in doubt.

Chapter 3: Shopping for an Operating System

In order for one computer to be compatible with another, both must use the same operating system. This is possible because several manufacturers make computers that run the same operating system. Manufacturers do this so their computers will have access to that operating system's software base and, therefore, will sell better.

So, even if your computer is made in the back of Fred's Compute-O-Rama, if it has the same (or even a similar) microprocessor and uses the same operating system as your computers at work, Fred's computer is considered compatible and has access to all the software that you use at work. Needless to say, this is a boon to Fred's business.

However, suppose that Fred's computers only have the same microprocessor as your work computers, yet they run something called Fred's Operating System (FOS). His computers are not compatible. The machines will not have access to the large software base available to other computers, and you really must question your motive for visiting Fred's place (unless Fred is a relative of yours).

Software, the microprocessor, the operating system, and you

Figure 3-1 illustrates how the three parts of your computer system work with you. The operating system is really at the center of everything. You tell it what to do. For example, you say, "Run my word processor," and the operating system does that. When you quit working with your word processor, the operating system takes over again, begging you to do something else.

19

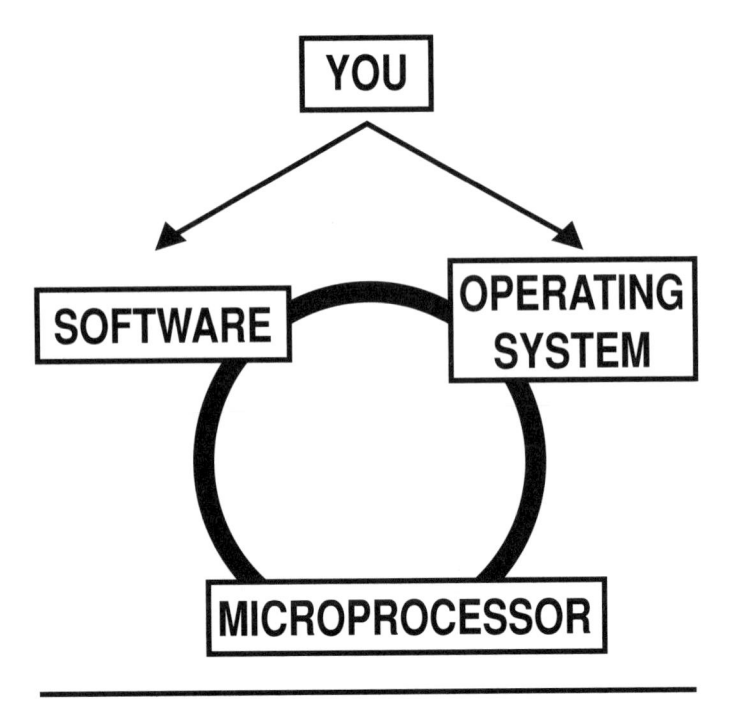

Figure 3-1: How your computer system works.

The operating system also plays an important role in carefully insulating you from the perils of controlling your computer hardware directly. In the olden days, computer owners actually had to throw rows upon rows of tiny switches to configure their computers. Today that chore is handled most adeptly by the operating system; with a good operating system, you'll never have to mess with the configuration of your computer, and if you do, it should be most pleasant.

Keep in mind that I said it *should* be most pleasant. There are different degrees of friendliness in computer operating systems. Some of them, well, you might as well have that row of tiny switches. Others let you comfortably control your computer with a minimum of fuss. I'll discuss which operating systems are hostile and which are friendly toward the end of this chapter, though Figure 3-2 should tell you where each one fits on the scale.

Chapter 3: Shopping for an Operating System

Macintosh | Windows | OS/2 | DOS | UNIX

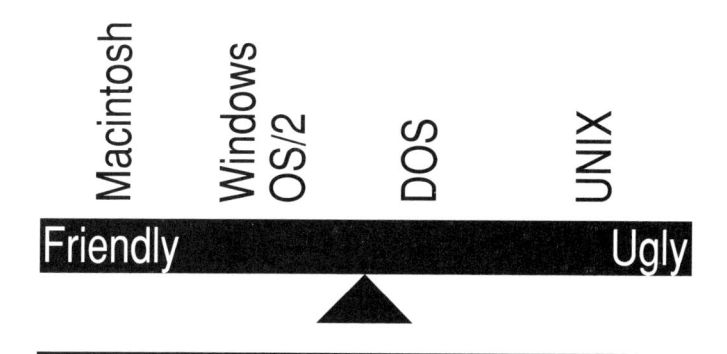

Friendly ——————————————————— Ugly

Figure 3-2: How operating systems weigh in on the friendliness scale.

"What the heck is the BIOS?"

Another key part to your computer is the *BIOS* (pronounced BYE-oss), an acronym for Basic Input/Output System. It works like an operating system but on a simple, or basic, level. The BIOS is responsible for making sure that all parts of the computer communicate with each other; it starts up the computer every time you turn on the power switch, and it also loads the operating system from disk.

A while back, a major deal was made over a computer's BIOS. In the early days of the IBM PC, compatible computers yearned to have a BIOS that worked just like IBM's — but without infringing upon IBM's copyrights. Some of those early systems lacked full compatibility, which meant they couldn't run all the IBM software, and lo, those computers became boat anchors. Today that isn't a problem; you'd have to look real hard to find a computer with a non-standard BIOS.

Incidentally, the BIOS is recorded on a *ROM* (Read-Only Memory) chip inside your computer. On some PCs, such as the Macintosh, the operating system is also recorded on a ROM chip. Most of the time, the operating system lives on a disk drive like other software.

21

Choosing an Operating System

In the old days, it was the computer you chose. Today you choose an operating system first. That's because the operating system is what "owns" all the software. You pick the right operating system, and its software base will follow. Only then do you look for the hardware to make everything run.

Your computer's operating system and software are closely related. They share a lot of characteristics. For example, some software is easy to use and some is not so easy. All operating systems have their equal share of programs that are easy and programs that aren't so easy; however, some operating systems are inherently easy, and therefore, their programs are generally easy too.

Not so easy. The DOS operating system is very popular and has thousands of programs available. But DOS is cryptic. It's text-only and ugly to look at. Most of the DOS software follows in this mold; you'll find it to be text-only and not very pretty. (Though there are pretty DOS programs and easy-to-use DOS programs.)

The OS/2 wild card

DOS and Windows aren't the only two operating systems in the universe. Another operating system, currently popular with about 4 million PC users, is *OS/2*.

The main problem with OS/2 is that it lacks specific, OS/2-only software, such as an OS/2 version of a popular word processor or spreadsheet. And I don't mean a cheap imitation, either. For OS/2 to succeed and, more importantly, be a worthy competitor with DOS and Windows, it needs software of its own — software that takes advantage of the power that OS/2 offers. Presently, that software doesn't exist. This means a lot of OS/2 users muddle along running DOS and Windows programs. If that's true, then it seems like there's really no reason to bother with OS/2.

Fairly easy. The Windows operating system is more friendly than DOS, and most of its programs tend to follow suit.

Mostly easy. The Macintosh operating system is even more friendly than Windows, and all its programs are very easy to get used to. Both Windows and the Macintosh operating systems are graphical in nature and tend to be more fun and interesting than something boring like DOS text.

Could be easy but tends to be technical. I'd rate the OS/2 operating system as being more technical than Windows but still not as technical as DOS. Although it is graphical and easy to use, OS/2 contains a lot of doodads and whatzits that please computer hackers but may get in the way of someone just passing by.

Not easy at all. And on the ultra cryptic end of the scale, there's the UNIX operating system, which is really ideal for computer scientists but more like being rubbed with sandpaper for the rest of us.

You may think to yourself that you need something easy to get used to. If so, great. Keep that in mind when you look for software. Confine yourself to an easy-to-learn operating system, and you'll find all the software there is easy as well.

✔ Quick Review

When it comes to buying a computer, software is more important than hardware. The most important software is the operating system, your PC's main control program.

Though you really don't need to shop for an operating system, you should gear your software shopping toward one operating system or another. This is primarily based on how much software is available for the operating system and how easy it is to use. That's about as detailed as you need to get for now. The rest will fall into place as you hunt for software, a topic covered in the following chapter.

CHAPTER 4

Shopping for Software

Looking for Those Programs That Will Get the Job Done

Looking for software is easy, once you know what it is that you want the computer to do. If you plan on writing, you'll need a word processor. If you're really into numbers and accounting (and exciting numeric stuff), a spreadsheet may be in your future. If you're into managing lists of items, people's names, an inventory, or the kinds of ants that now call your house "home," a database will suit you. Artists will love drawing and painting programs. And your kids (and, yes, you too) will love the games . . . er, entertainment programs you can buy. Whatever the job, you now have to find the proper software.

How to Buy Software

The first step to buying software is to know what it is you want. This chapter introduces you to the various software categories out there and explains what to look for in each one. But before heading off to the Mr. Software store, you should know what it is you're about to do.

Taking the test-drive

Buying software is a matter of taste, like discovering new food. You should sit down at a computer and try out any software that you plan on buying. Any store that sells software should let you do this. All you need to do is ask, "Can I try out the Crunchy Spreadsheet, please?" As a buyer, you're entitled to go on a test-drive.

If the store doesn't let you try the software, then go somewhere else. Tell the sales folk that you're a serious shopper and that you won't be in again. But I believe you'll find that most stores will be more than happy to help set you up. Don't feel guilty about asking, either.

Obviously you can't be an expert in any software package you pick out. If possible, ask for a demonstration, but be sure they allow you time to play with the software.

What should you look for? Look for things you like. If the software is a word processor, how easy is it for you to start typing? Do the various things on the screen look obvious to you? Is it cryptic? Does it feel slow or awkward? Make a note of these things and if the word processor doesn't meet with your liking, try another. You should apply this technique to all software that you test-drive.

Helpful hints

"User-friendly" is one of the biggest myths of the computer industry. Try as the industry must, the stuff never really gets easy to use. In fact, if they try to make it easy, it usually winds up being inane or boring. Still, looking for friendly software now will avoid any confusion later.

> ### Other sources for test-driving
>
> Having a computer-knowledgeable friend can be a boost to picking out some good software. Let your friend show you some of his or her favorite software packages. This is how I got started a dozen or so years ago — I basically used everything my "computer guru" was using on his computer. It wasn't what I ended up using, but it was a good start.
>
> If you live in an area without software stores, you'll have to rely heavily on other sources. Appendix B lists some sources containing additional information about where you can look up software reviews or consult with computer people about what to buy.
>
> Another tactic some people use is to look at what's popular. If you live out in the boonies (like I do), then call up a mail-order place and ask what sells best. For example, "What's the best-selling database for a philatelist like me?" Then have the salesperson read the requirements from the side of the box for you. The salesperson might also be able to fax you information, should you have access to a fax machine.

Even if the software doesn't claim to be user-friendly (which the industry likes to call *user-hostile*), check out its *help features*. A help feature allows you to press a special key or choose a menu item to display helpful hints while you're using the program. A few programs lack help features, assuming the manual is so totally enlightening that you won't need them, but having a program that offers help is a bonus.

Don't forget support!

No one wants to be stranded when buying anything — especially when buying something for a computer. That's why you want to make sure that someone's going to be available when you need help. In this case, you should expect support from both the store where you bought the software and the software developer.

Software stores can offer help as far as returning defective merchandise and offering advice. Occasionally they have classes, or they can steer you in the direction of good instruction. They also have computer books, which I can't recommend enough! Beyond that, you should check your software package to see what kind of support the publisher offers. It can really vary.

Types of help you'll find in software

Those programs nice enough to offer help provide it in two varieties: *on-line help* and *contextual help*.

On-line help. This means that wherever you are in the program, you can press a special key and see a list of commands or a copy of the manual. This type of help is good for looking up topics or seeing how things are done.

Contextual help. This is the same kind of help as on-line help, except that the helpful information you see will pertain to whatever you're currently doing in the program. For example, if you're about to print, the helpful information is about printing. If you're about to save something onto disk, the helpful information is about saving, and so on.

27

Some software manufacturers offer telephone support for when you really get stuck. With phone support, you can actually call up the company and directly ask them questions about the software. However, phone support comes in three flavors: vanilla, chocolate, and fudge. These are my flavors, by the way — not an industry standard (well, maybe in the ice cream industry).

Vanilla. Vanilla phone support means you pay not only for the phone call, but for the support as well. When the software developers answer the phone, they usually greet you with, "Hi! What's your credit card number?" These software houses charge upwards of $60/hour just so you can ask them questions about their product. (Customer Service Rest in Peace.) But for the fancier user-hostile packages, many find this price agreeable.

Chocolate. Chocolate support is better than vanilla. With this kind of phone support you pay only for the phone call. Once you get connected, you simply wait on hold until someone happens by to answer your question. The answer is free; it's just that most of these places tend to be long-distance.

Fudge. Fudge phone support is the best. With this kind of support, you get an 800 number — a free phone call — for free support. The only drawback is that these numbers are busy . . . a lot.

Take note of the kind of support offered by the developer of the software you've chosen. If it's not on the box, then ask the salesperson what the support is like.

Other flavors of support

The most common type of support available right now is kind of Neapolitan. That means it's a little fudge, a little chocolate, and a little vanilla. For example, you may get "free" support for 90 days after buying your product. But after that, you must pay a fee to talk with someone.

And after you find what you want...

When you feel you've found a software package that will help you get your work done a lot easier, make a note of it. Fill in the forms at the front of this book describing the software you've found to get the job done. (Feel free to photocopy the forms so that you'll have a few of them.)

After you've found your software, wait. This isn't buying-time right now. Your next step is to find the hardware to match the software you've selected. For now, keep your software worksheets handy.

By the way, if you haven't checked out other packages or they weren't in stock, then make a note of them as well. The idea is to keep track of what you need versus what you've played with so far. Go back to the store when the other stuff is in stock so you can check it out as well.

Eventually you'll find everything you need. Then it's time to do a little homework that will make buying the computer hardware a lot easier.

Looking at the Software Box

Software comes in a box. Inside the box are the disks, the infamous manual that supposedly contains instructions and opinions on using the software, and other goodies such as registration cards, keyboard templates, bumper stickers, buttons, and more sheets of paper than you ever found in a Publisher's Clearinghouse giveaway.

On the side of the box are the "nutritional requirements" of the software. You should find a list of the equipment that the software requires. Typically, you'll find answers to the following questions:

1. Which computer is required?
2. Which operating system is required?
3. Which microprocessor is required?
4. How much memory (RAM) is needed?
5. How much hard drive space is needed?
6. Which type of graphics is required?
7. Is any sound equipment or multimedia support offered?
8. What kind of printers are supported?
9. What kind of support is offered?

There may be even more questions about even more confusing issues. Don't let that boggle you now! The subject of hardware is discussed in Chapters 6 through 12 of this book. (If you do find it confusing, then by all means, read those chapters before you visit the software store.)

The previous questions are designed to make sure that you buy a software package that your computer can handle. Some computers are too weak to be able to deal with some software. Or you could say that the software is really demanding, but since you haven't bought your computer yet, the idea is to make sure that whatever you buy matches the appetite of your software. So far, you're sitting pretty.

> ### Things to look out for in software descriptions
>
> Now, before getting all excited, there are a few warnings you should bear in mind when reading the information on the side of a software box.
>
> If the word *recommended* is used, beware! For example, it may say it requires 3MB of RAM, but 10MB is recommended. Usually this means you *need* 10MB or the product won't perform up to expectations.
>
> Also, avoid version 1.0 of a program. Version 1.0 is the first release of any program and it's bound to have some boo-boos in it (programmers like to call them *bugs*). Version 1.1, 1.2, and so on are fairly proven and bug-free. Also, the higher the version number (1 is the version number in 1.2; 2 is the release number), the longer the program has been around and the more proven it is.

Reading a software box

- MS-DOS operating system Version 5.0 or later
- 386/25 or higher microprocessor (486 or higher recommended)
- 550K of conventional memory and 768K of expanded memory
- High-density disk drive
- 320 x 400 x 256 color VGA or higher resolution color monitor (Super VGA recommended)
- Microsoft Mouse or compatible pointing device recommended
- Sound board recommended
- Compatible with joystick

Above is a copy of information that you may find on the side of a box of software — just like nutritional information on the side of a cereal box. It's important to know how to read this information to see if your computer can run this software — or to see what items the computer that you're planning on buying should have. For example, in the preceding list you have the following:

1. This software requires DOS Version 5.0 or later.

2. This software requires a 386 microprocessor running at 25 MHz, though if I were you, I'd have a 486 or it will run as slow as a slug.

3. This software requires all your conventional memory and a lot of expanded memory (see Chapter 7 for definitions). Better have 2MB of memory in your computer.

4. You need a 1.44MB or 1.2MB floppy disk drive.

5. The software requires VGA graphics, though you should have Super VGA to get the thrill of it all.

6. The software needs a mouse.

7. The software works much better with a sound board.

8. If you have a joystick, you can use it with this software.

✔ Quick Review

The most important thing to remember about software is that it controls the hardware. The reason you buy a particular kind of computer is to run a particular kind of software package.

When you look for software, be sure to test-drive it. Examine the features. See if the level of help is to your liking. And find out how well the product is supported by the manufacturer (vanilla, chocolate, and so on). Then write down information about the software on the worksheets provided at the front of this book.

The next chapter goes into a little more detail on the kinds of software available.

CHAPTER 5

The Software Cavalcade

■ ■

Everything You Wanted to Know about Software (But Were Afraid to Ask)

Your computer needs software like an orchestra needs a conductor, like a car needs a driver, like an actor needs a script — you get the idea. So far, your quest for the perfect personal computer has had you examine your needs and has prepared you to hunt for software. May the hunt begin!

Even though you may have heard the terms tossed around, the information in this chapter properly describes the more popular categories of software and what each one does. Odds are really good that you'll be picking one or more of the following types of software, depending on your needs, likes, and whims.

Word processors

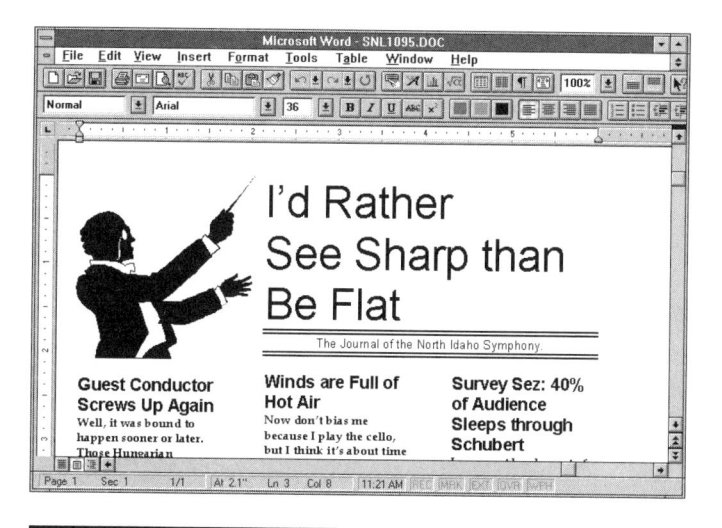

Figure 5-1: Graphics and text are combined in this word processor.

33

A word processor (shown in Figure 5-1) is like an electronic typewriter. You can enter and edit text right on your computer's screen. Words can be changed, moved, inserted, and deleted all with a few keystrokes. (But don't let the ads fool you. Owning a word processor only makes writing easier; it does not make you a better writer.)

Contemporary word processors include an armada of writing tools, from an electronic spell-check program to a grammar checker to tools that will actually write some things for you automatically. These are all handy features to have, but word processors are also notorious for including features you may not need.

For example, one popular word processing package has lots of tools for lawyers. Are you a lawyer? If not, then you're paying for that stuff even though you don't use it. The truth is, most people — myself included — only use about 20 percent of the bonus features in their word processors.

Ideally, you want a word processor that allows you to do your writing job. In fact, you may want one of the *simple* word processors and not the big brand names. Please don't let the salesmen steer you towards something you don't need. Tell them you don't want to pay for a lot of features you'll never use, and don't fall sucker to their line, "But what if one day you *do* need that automatic hat-checking feature?".

Spreadsheets

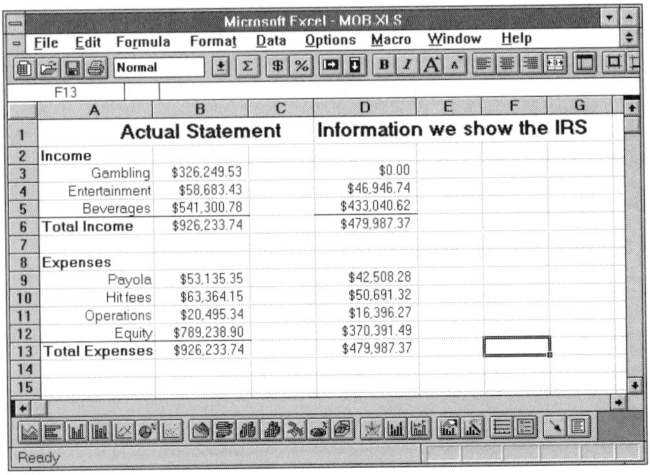

Figure 5-2: Spreadsheets make toying with numbers easy.

CHAPTER 5: THE SOFTWARE CAVALCADE

> ### The desktop publishing category
>
> An offshoot from word processing is *desktop publishing*. This is where you combine words and pictures and create a *layout* of your finished page; for example, you could create a pamphlet, a church bulletin, or even a novel.
>
> Many word processors incorporate desktop publishing features as part of their design. They allow you to mix different typestyles on-screen so that you can see in advance exactly what the printout will look like. This style of word processor is called *WYSIWYG* (pronounced *wizzy-wig*), which stands for What-You-See-Is-What-You-Get. You can even add graphics to your text to really spice things up.
>
> For desktop publishing in particular, you usually need separate word processing and graphics software. If you're into this, make sure that the desktop publishing package recognizes your word processing and graphics software.

Spreadsheet programs play with numbers (see Figure 5-2). By using a spreadsheet, you can manipulate, examine, and change numeric values and their relationships to other values, but it's really not that boring.

Used primarily for business applications, spreadsheets allow you to design an electronic balance sheet or general ledger for your company. You can also manipulate various figures and instantly see how other figures are affected. You can, for example, see how it's possible to embezzle funds without anyone noticing!

Spreadsheets have come a long way since the old days of *VisiCalc* (the galaxy's first spreadsheet). A full-featured spreadsheet should be capable of *windowing*, or showing multiple areas of the spreadsheet at one time; sorting figures; linking information between two or more spreadsheets; and creating graphs. Nothing spices up a dull meeting like some pie charts and bar graphs.

Databases

People use a database program to manipulate information, such as a listing of your record collection or a tally of unruly employees. Any time you have a list of items, it's a good idea to place the list into a computer's database for manipulation. Names, addresses, and telephone numbers are the most common items that find their way into a database. In fact, an entire industry exists that thrives on collecting and selling names and addresses (just in case you didn't know).

A good database program will have a number of features available. The program should be able to look quickly through all the information in a list and pick out those items you want. For example, suppose you're a vampire and your database contains all the types of blood in your blood cellar. If you want a particular blood type, Rh, color, year, and vintage, you simply inform your database. It should then locate the exact pint you desire.

Variations on a database theme

You may not believe it, but there are more database programs out there than anything else. The major packages are more like programming languages; they let you create your own database and write a teeny program that somehow controls it. These are for the die-hards. For everyone else, customized database programs can be found in abundance. For example, you may find an address program for keeping track of your friends and contacts that can also print mailing labels. Another popular example is personal-organizer software, which includes an address list, appointment calendar, and other goodies.

Home-budgeting software

Spreadsheets are fine for the home, but what you probably need is some type of home-budgeting software. These programs can do more than just balance your checkbook or print your checks (with the proper check-like paper). They can track investments and loans and even make forecasts. Several popular packages exist, and all of them are quick to learn and easy to use.

CHAPTER 5: THE SOFTWARE CAVALCADE

Graphics

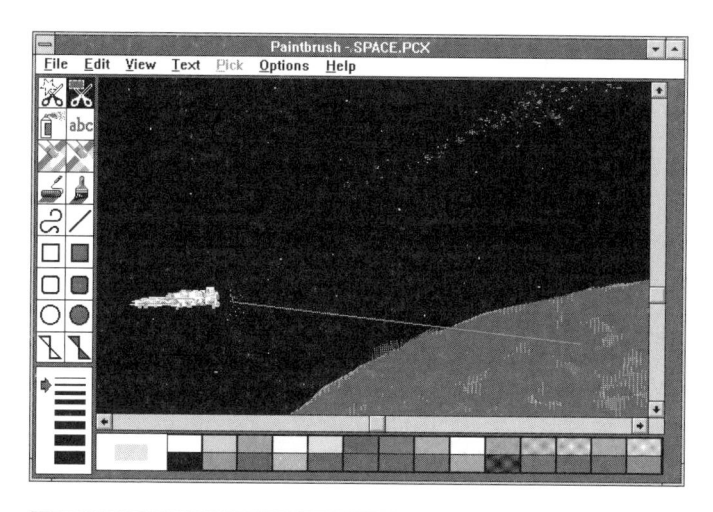

Figure 5-3: Painting programs make your computer an artist.

Graphics software falls into two categories: *drawing programs* and *painting programs*. These programs allow you to create and manipulate a graphic image on the screen. Drawing programs, also known as *CAD* (for Computer Assisted Design), are much more precise than painting programs. CAD deals with *objects* rather than dots on the screen. Painting programs are more recreational and not as accurate as CAD (see Figure 5-3).

If you're an engineer or architect, you'll probably be spending some serious bucks for a decent graphics system. Graphics software and the required computer components can get expensive. However, once the information is in the computer, making a change involves only manipulating a few objects on the screen, pressing a key, and — presto! — a new copy is printed without your having to visit the drafting table.

If you're going to get into graphics, I strongly recommend that you buy your computer a mouse. That's a *computer* mouse. Although your computer may enjoy having its own *live* pet mouse, this won't help you with your graphics programs. Your computer will also need lots of memory and sophisticated graphics — but this you'll learn from reading the software box as discussed in the preceding chapter.

37

BUY THAT COMPUTER! 1995 EDITION

Communications Software

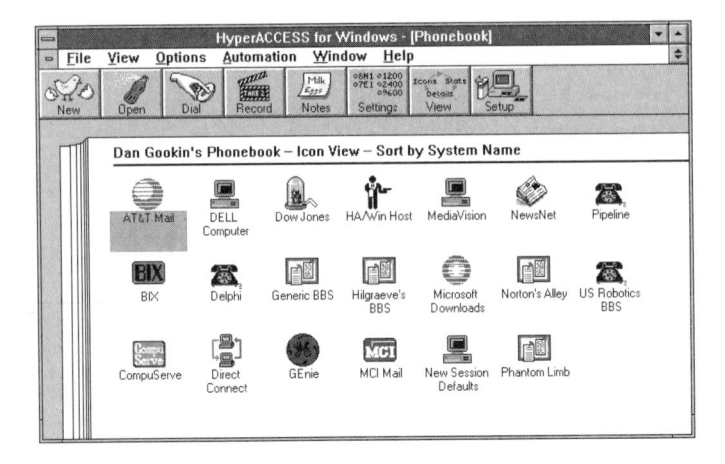

Figure 5-4: Communications programs let your computer talk to other computers using a modem.

Communications software, shown in Figure 5-4, allows your computer to take advantage of a *modem* and the phone system to talk with other computers. This area of software is rather crude when compared with the sophistication and ease of use in the other categories. In fact, most communications software packages come free when you purchase your modem, so you won't have to make your own choice.

> ### Maddening modem software
>
> There are lots and lots of software packages that make use of your modem. Most commonly, you'll probably use a general communications program, or *telcom* program.
>
> If you're interested in using one of the major on-line services available, such as Prodigy or America Online, you'll have to buy software that works specifically with those services. The software will still use your modem, but only by using that software can you call Prodigy or America Online. Other on-line services, such as CompuServe and GEnie, may offer their own software as well. And for riding on the *Internet*, there are specific packages you can buy — even more stuff still! (In fact, I have over a dozen modem/communications programs on my computer!)

Recreation

Games. This whole personal computer craze really started with the home arcade game of the early '80s. There are computer games available for every computer on the market. Some computers, those with advanced graphics and sound capabilities, make the best game machines. Without sound and graphics, you might as well buy a Nintendo.

Many different types of computer games are available. There are arcade-style shoot-'em-ups; classics like Chess, Go, and Othello; text adventure games; *little man* games ala PacMan; and simulation games, such as flight simulators, war simulators, and business simulators. The *creativity well* never runs dry with computer games.

Education

Educational software is more available for some types of computers than others. Popular computers will always have educational software. However, computers geared toward graphics and sound have a stronger appeal to kids than do business machines. (In fact, if you're concerned about which computer to get your children, get the same one they're using in school.)

Educational software also tends to be expensive and risky. You never really know what you're getting into until you buy. It's strongly recommended that you check software reviews in magazines or ask teachers what's best as far as educational software goes.

Utilities

A special category of software is the *utility* program (as shown in Figure 5-5). These programs differ from the other ones mentioned in this chapter in that they aren't used for productivity. A utility program doesn't do your work on the computer; it works on the computer itself. Typically, a utility program will do one of three things: improve performance, diagnose a problem, or repair something that's wrong.

```
(C:\) undelete

UNDELETE - A delete protection facility
Copyright (C) 1987-1993 Central Point Software, Inc.
All rights reserved.
Directory: C:\
File Specifications: *.*

    Delete Sentry control file not found.

    Deletion-tracking file not found.

    MS-DOS directory contains    19 deleted files.
    Of those,    19 files may be recovered.

Using the MS-DOS directory method.

      ?OCBBJAH            1835 10-28-94  2:33p  ...A  Undelete (Y/N)?
```

Figure 5-5: Another lost file is rescued thanks to an undelete utility.

Utilities come in bundles of several dozen programs. For example, one program may recover files you deleted, another may rescue a damaged hard drive, another may optimize the way your PC uses memory. Other utility-like programs include calculators, appointment books, little word processors (called *text editors*), and so on.

Programming

```
≡  File  Edit  Search  Run  Compile  Debug  Project  Options  Window  Help
┌─[■]──────────────────────────── CRAPS.C ──────────────────────────2=[↕]┐
│void main()                                                              │
│{                                                                        │
│        int x,YouWannaPlay,pot,bet,point;                                │
│        char c;                                                          │
│                                                                         │
│/* Setup */                                                              │
│        seedrnd();                    //randomizer                       │
│        printf("\nVegas Craps!\nThe dice game no one understands.\n\n"); │
│        YouWannaPlay=TRUE;                                               │
│        pot=100;                      //start with $100                  │
│                                                                         │
│/* Play the game main loop*/                                             │
│        while(YouWannaPlay)                                              │
│           {                                                             │
│/* First get their bet in a do-while loop. The bet must be               │
│greater than $2 and can't be greater than their pot (total).             │
│If the bet is less than 2, the if statement displays a rude              │
│message. */                                                              │
│           do                                                            │
│              {                                                          │
│                      printf("You have $%i in your pot.\n",pot);         │
│───── 1:1 ═════◄▌                                                    ►   │
│ F1 Help  F2 Save  F3 Open  Alt-F9 Compile  F9 Make  F10 Menu            │
```

Figure 5-6: By writing your own program, you can tell the computer what to do.

Programming languages allow you to write and run your own computer software (see Figure 5-6). Many programming languages are available, some easy to learn, some hard. You don't need to be good at math to learn a programming language, either. Just having a healthy curiosity about computers helps.

Most of the popular programming languages are available for all types of computers. Of them, the only two worth bothering with are C (or C++) and BASIC.

C (pronounced *see*) isn't easy, but it's the most popular computer programming language and most of the software you buy is written in the C language. There are many C language *compilers* available, though. You also need to buy a few good books on the subject if you plan to do anything useful.

The BASIC programming language is the easiest to learn, probably since it most resembles English (though *most* is stretching it a bit). The most popular variations of BASIC are the QuickBASIC and VisualBASIC programs available from Microsoft.

Other languages are available as well, each of them with its own army of followers and individual charms and detractions.

Learning how to program your computer makes you feel more confident when you use it. As you program the machine, you learn more about it. And the best part about learning how to program is that you can write interesting applications for yourself. As an example, I've written a stupid little program in BASIC that prints out my name and address on mailing labels. I now never need to fill out the return address on my bills. When I need more labels, I just run the program again.

Multimedia Software

Multimedia is a term used to cover a wide variety of programs available for your computer. Basically, these programs use graphics and sound to present information or entertain you (see Figure 5-7).

I suppose the common ground for multimedia software is that it comes on a CD-ROM, which means your computer will need a CD-ROM drive plus sound and graphics abilities. (See Chapter 12.)

Figure 5-7: A complete encyclopedia on CD-ROM.

One of the most interesting aspects of multimedia software is that it can be interactive. For example, you don't just read about how an internal combustion engine works in a multimedia encyclopedia — you actually see it working on the screen. You can also see video clips of famous events, hear strange musical instruments, and enjoy interesting animation right on your computer screen.

Software for Free

Believe it or not, not all software costs money. In fact, a good number of programs are available for free or almost free. Some software may come *free* with your computer; some may be available from nice people who write software and give it away because they're eccentric geniuses and expect their rewards in the hereafter.

Please keep in mind that, though there is software available for nothing to next-to-nothing, not all software is free. Don't accept software that you know can be purchased at the store from a well-meaning friend who's giving it away. This is theft. Only if the software states that it's free (or a *demo*) can you legally use it without paying.

CHAPTER 5: THE SOFTWARE CAVALCADE

> ### And on the way to the check out counter, let me just throw this in...
>
> A classic trick of the slimier computer salespeople is to *throw in* software with your computer purchase. Watch out! You've been had!
>
> Never figure the cost of your computer with software thrown in *for free*. Always get a price quote without any software (except for the operating system, which should be included). Use that quote for comparison shopping. Figure on paying for your software later as a separate purchase or just have them calculate the costs separately.

Public domain software

Another type of free software is known as *public domain*. These software packages are written by little men in small rooms who stay up all night and think philanthropic thoughts. They program their brains out and then give away the software. Most of the public domain software packages are games. Occasionally, however, some really nice *major league* programs rise up from the swamp.

Shareware

Another type of *free* software is referred to as *shareware*. This software is distributed free of charge, just like public domain software. The exception is that if you use and enjoy the program, the author requests that you send a donation.

Most programs labeled public domain actually fall into the shareware category. Usually, when you're done using a shareware program, a guilt message will flash on the screen, urging you to send the poor, starving programmer some money.

43

Demo software

A final category of free software is the demo program. These are software programs that are available for money, though they've created a special version that allows you to *try before you buy*. Simply set up the demo software on your computer, use it, decide if you like it, and then buy it. That's the idea, anyway.

Demo software is usually crippled in some way. For example, a demo word processor may not print or save files to disk. This is why it's free; they want you to buy the real version so you can print and save your stuff to disk. (Without those features, the software is fairly useless; but for *just-looking*, it's great.)

Bundled Software

Some computers come with *bundled software* when you buy them. A classic example was the old Kaypro CP/M computer. For years, Kaypro gave away software with every computer — you got everything you needed all at once. The software usually included a word processor, spreadsheet, and a database; and for the most part, the software was very good — often of the same quality you'd buy separately, only free!

Today, bundled software is still given away, though not as many individual packages as before. You should expect to get your operating system for free with your computer. Consider anything else a bonus.

Integrated Versus Stand-Alone Software

The last major kind of software is referred to as *integrated*. This is where a software vendor combines the capabilities of several kinds of software and stuffs them all into one package. The thinking behind integrated software is, "Why buy three packages for your computer when one will suit all your needs?". The drawback is that when the software tries to be a jack-of-all-trades, it usually winds up mastering none.

There are many pluses and minuses to integrated software. The first plus is that you only need to learn one program. Usually, the commands for the word processor are the same or similar to those used by the spreadsheet and database, and information is easily shared among them. Also, you pay less for one integrated program than you would for three separate items (though integrated software *is* notoriously expensive).

The disadvantages of integrated software are that often each integrated program — word processor, database, and so on — lacks the power of a stand-alone program. And sometimes the integrated package contains features you really don't need or won't ever use. You still pay for those features whether you want them or not. For getting started, however, an integrated package can be a good choice.

Meanwhile, back at the *office* type of integrated program

A popular tactic for major software vendors is to distribute the *office* integrated package of software — for example, Microsoft Office, SmartSuite (Lotus), and PerfectOffice (WordPerfect). These packages come with a real word processor, database, spreadsheet, and so on. They aren't cheapie versions either; the vendors just combine all their top-selling stuff and sell it for a lower price in a bundle.

There is no problem with buying this type of integrated software. A minor drawback is that the packages really aren't that similar (since they were combined in a box and not truly integrated). But the major drawback comes at upgrading time.

After a year to six months, most software developers come out with a newer, better version of their programs. The cost of upgrading each one, especially when you have an *office,* can be outrageous.

✔ Quick Review

Armed with the knowledge you gained from this chapter and the previous one, you're ready to go scouting for your software.

Remember to fill in the card at the front of this book as you discover which software you like. This will help you assemble the proper computer for your needs, and it makes the hardware shopping phase a lot easier.

Oh, and one thing no one expects is that software is expensive. Plan on spending almost as much on software as you've set aside for your computer purchase . So if you have budgeted $1,500 for your computer, you'll probably end up spending that on software, too.

Don't be alarmed! It's not necessary to purchase all your software at once. In fact, I recommend against it. Instead, buy only one or two packages — the core of what you need. Then take them home with your new computer and learn them. When you're ready to buy more software, then buy it. There's no need weighing yourself down with a lot of software right away.

Chapter 6

The Microprocessor

■■■■■■■■■■■■■■■■■■■■■■■■■■■■■■

Choosing the Most Important Part of Your Computer System

At the center of everything in your computer's hardware is the microprocessor. It's your PC's main control chip, and just about everything else you have in your computer depends on the capabilities of the microprocessor.

Without even getting into the boring details, I can tell you that the best microprocessor — the one you *really* want — is the latest, fastest, and most expensive model. But that's what you want. What you *need* can be a different story entirely, one that this chapter explains with all the detail and trimmings.

Hardware pieces parts

There are many different parts to a computer. The following is a brief list of those items you'll find in and around a computer, listed in order of importance.

Inside the computer:

- Microprocessor (also known as *CPU* or the *processor*)
- Computer memory (*RAM*)
- Hard drive(s)
- Floppy drive(s)
- Busses and ports

Outside the computer:

- Monitor
- Keyboard and mouse
- Printer
- Modems and fax/modems
- Multimedia paraphernalia
- Other stuff

Each of these items is covered in this chapter and the chapters that follow.

47

The Microprocessor

Some people claim that a computer's microprocessor is its brain. Actually, it's not as gooey as that. And the term *brain* is highly inaccurate; there is no native intelligence inside a computer. You must have software to tell the microprocessor what to do. That still doesn't undermine its importance as the number one, big cheese chip in your computer.

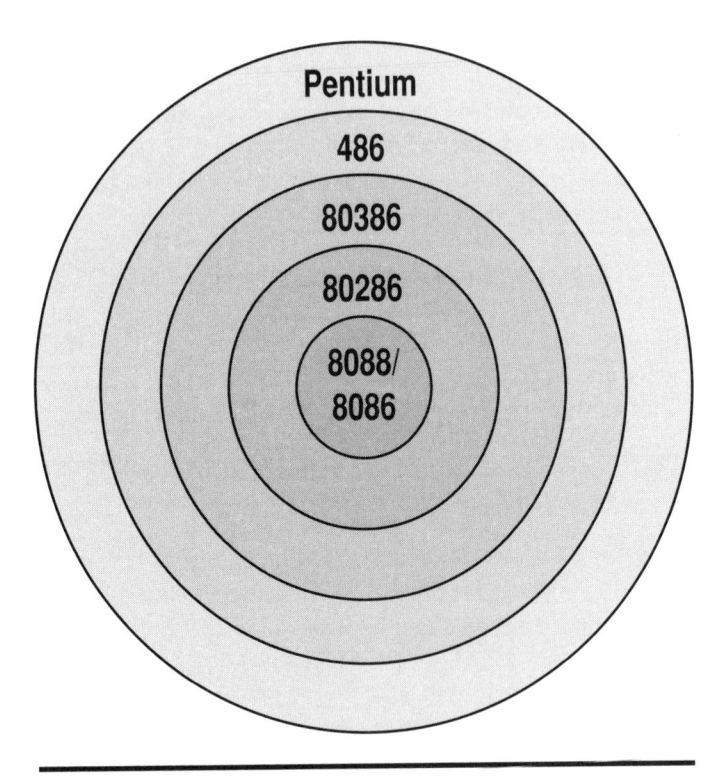

Figure 6-1: The microprocessor target.

The microprocessor itself is a silicon chip on which thousands or even millions of circuits are etched. The microprocessor will also be called a CPU, for Central Processing Unit, or just "the processor." All terms refer to the same thing. Remember the terms, or just that they're the same.

Microprocessors are judged by three factors:

- Number/name
- Bit width (power)
- Megahertz (speed)

Microprocessor names and numbers

Each processor chip is referred to by a number. The engineers who create the chips are fond of naming things after numbers: their cars, dogs, children, and so on. Processor numbers aren't sequentially named. Instead, they're grouped into *families*. Typical processor names are the 80486, the 68020, the 80386, the 6908, the 65C816, and so on. You get the idea.

IBM computers and their ilk use the 80x86 microprocessor family. The *x* in the number is replaced by other numbers, depending on how recently the processor chip was developed. The numbers really don't hold any true meaning, however; what you need to understand is that processors of the same family tree can understand each other.

For example, a processor that is a descendant of, or similar to, another processor can read and understand the same software written for the original processor. So a program written with instructions for the 80386 processor will work on a computer using the 80486 processor. Even though the 80486 is a more advanced chip, it still understands the language of its ancestor, the 80386. (See Figure 6-1, the microprocessor target chart, earlier in this chapter.)

Processors from different family trees, however, cannot understand each other. The instructions that are used to tell a Macintosh's 68030 processor to "walk the dog" will not be understood by an 80386. This is yet another reason why it's important to read the side of a software box before you buy a program.

Another important thing to remember with processor numbers is that the larger the number gets, the more recent the chip. The more recent chips (larger numbers) are considered the *offspring* of the older chips. So an 80486 chip is later and better than an 80386 chip, since 4 is bigger than 3.

The only exception to the numbering madness is the new PC microprocessor chip, which Intel chose to call the *Pentium* instead of the 80586. The reason was that they couldn't trademark a number, so they dreamt up a new name instead. (In reality, the *Pentium* chip is really just an 80586, or a 586.)

> ### The Pentium is hot!
>
> Considering a Pentium microprocessor? Then you should know that they're *hot*. And I don't mean selling well or popular; I'm referring to the chip's running temperature. A Pentium microprocessor, on and running, can get so hot that you can't touch it with your finger. Because of this, it's very important that you buy a Pentium computer with a microprocessor cooling fan. It sounds cute, and it is; the little fan sits on top of the microprocessor chip and keeps it cool, which means your computer will run more efficiently. So always insist on getting a good quality fan, one that will last as long as you hope your Pentium computer will.

Measuring power, or bit width

A microprocessor's power is measured by its *bit width*. That's the number of bits the microprocessor can digest at once. The bigger the number, the more the microprocessor is capable of and the more powerful it is. For example, a 32-bit microprocessor can eat information in 32-bit chunks. That's twice as much (and twice as fast) as a microprocessor that's only 16 bits.

> ### Is it an 80386? 386? 386SX? 386DX? What's going on?
>
> Computer people love numbers (if you haven't guessed already). And big numbers, well, they're just hard to say over and over at the office. So to cut down on the idle chit-chat between engineers, computer marketing people started referring to chips by their nicknames. To wit:
>
> - 80286 is really a 286 (two-eighty-six).
> - 80386 is really a 386 (three-eighty-six).
> - 80486 is really 486 and sometimes an i486 (eye-four-eighty-six).
> - 80586 is really a *Pentium*.
>
> The SX, DX, DX2, and other suffixes refer to how the chip was constructed internally. You'll read about it in the upcoming section titled "Speed and megahertz."

> ### The SX connection
>
> One caveat with bit width exists for any 80386 microprocessor ending with SX, such as the 80386SX. That chip actually has two bit widths. The first is internal, the second is external.
>
> Internally, a 386SX chip digests information in large, 32-bit chunks. Externally, the chip communicates with the rest of the computer in only 16-bit chunks. This makes the SX microprocessor slower than the plain DX (which is the suffix for a full bit-width microprocessor), but it makes it cheaper. Also, the SX consumes less power, which is why you'll find it in a lot of laptop computers.
>
> The 486SX isn't like the 386SX as far as bit width is concerned. Instead, the 486SX lacks a few features of the full 486, or 486DX chip. Refer to the sidebar on *math coprocessors* for more information.

It helps to think of bit widths like cylinders in a car. The more cylinders, the more gutsy the car. A ten-cylinder Dodge Viper can go from 0 to 60 MPH in under three seconds. The old three-cylinder Chevy Sprint was so weak you had to use reverse gear to get up any hill in San Francisco — backwards!

Speed and megahertz

Processors also have a speed rating. Each chip whizzes along at a specific, regulated speed measured in *megahertz,* which is abbreviated as *MHz*. The higher the MHz value, the faster the chip. And the faster the chip, the more expensive it is.

Keep in mind that different speeds exist for the same microprocessor name. For example, you can have a 33 MHz 486 and a 50 MHz 486. The 50 MHz chip will do everything the 33 MHz chip will do — but much faster. Needless to say, the faster chip will also be much more expensive.

Megahertz also plays a role in some of the suffixes you'll see on microprocessor names. For example, a DX2 means that the microprocessor has two speeds. The one advertised, such as 66 MHz, is the fast speed the microprocessor uses internally. Externally, the chip communicates at half that speed, or 33 MHz for the example.

There's nothing wrong with a DX2 chip. It's not like the old 386SX microprocessor, which uses half the bit width. No, instead here it's speed, measured in MHz, and not power.

Also there is the DX3. These microprocessors run even faster than the DX2 and plain DX models. For example, a DX may run at 100 MHz, but only 33 MHz internally. (It's a very fast microprocessor.)

What about those "math coprocessors"?

A *math coprocessor* is a special companion chip for the microprocessor, kind of like a pocket calculator. Its job is to do mathematical computations, and it's engineered to do them more swiftly than the microprocessor can on its own.

Math coprocessors are only needed by those programs that require them, such as mathematical and design programs; if it doesn't say it needs a math coprocessor on the side of the box, then the software doesn't use one.

The 486 and Pentium-compatible microprocessors have a built-in math coprocessor chip. However, for 80386 and earlier microprocessors, you need to buy a companion math coprocessor separately if you need one.

My computer's faster than yours! Nya! Nya! Nya!

Computer speed ratings are a complete and total joke, though advertisers love to boast how much faster their model is than another, and you'll see bar graphs and charts in the magazines when they compare computer speeds. The truth is that speed is relative, because the computer sits around idle most of the time waiting for you to type something. Anyway, the following is a list of the various speed rating tests and what they mean, if anything.

Continued on next page →

Norton SI. The original computer speed rating, where a 1.0 equals the speed of the first IBM PC. The bigger the number, the faster the computer; however, the speed rating directly depends on the microprocessor's horsepower and not the computer's actual performance (meaning this test can be fooled).

Whetstones. A speed test that measures how fast the computer can do math (which the nerds call *floating point operations*). This test is somewhat inconsistent, so the punnish *Dhrystone* test is often used instead.

Dhrystones. A real-world test of a computer's performance. Instead of just measuring processor speed (like *Norton SI*), this test is a much better judge of how fast the computer will perform. Unfortunately, it too can be fooled.

Sieve of Eratosthenes. A mathematical test where a computer goes out and hunts down prime numbers. The time the computer takes is used as a gauge of its performance. This test is most like the *Norton SI* test in that its results don't really reflect how you use the computer; it's only a raw speed measurement.

Winstones. A test of a computer's ability to run Windows. This test, and other tests starting with "Win" (WinBench, Graphics Winmark, and so on) are specific to Windows. Some are geared toward its graphical performance, others measure the time it takes Windows to do things, which is a good judge of how the computer will perform in the real world.

The term *benchmark* is used to describe what these tests are measuring. So when you hear it used, know that it refers to a computer's performance as measured by some artificial test. Your mileage, as usual, will vary.

Microprocessors, memory, and madness

The type of microprocessor your computer has plays a direct role in how much memory you can install in your PC. This isn't as much of an issue as it was in the early days of the computer; back then, some computers could only have a small amount of memory because their microprocessors couldn't "see" a whole lot of memory. Today's microprocessors (see Table 6-1) can access far more memory than you'd ever need — or could afford!

Table 6-1 Microprocessors, Bit Width, Megahertz, and Memory (in Megabytes)

Micro-processor	A.K.A.	MHz (range)	Bit Width	Memory
8088/8086	V20, V30	4.77 - 8	8/16	1M
80286	286	6 - 20	16	16M
80386	386, 386SX	16-33	16/32	4,096M
486	80486, i486	25-100	32	4,096M
Pentium	586, 80586, P5	60-100+	32	4,096M

All about the cache

Another, more obscure attribute of a microprocessor is something called the *cache*, pronounced *cash*. A cache is a storage place. In a microprocessor, the cache is used to store instructions given the computer from a software program. The larger the cache storage area, the faster the microprocessor will go.

Occasionally, you may see a cache value used when describing a microprocessor. For example, the salesguy may boast that his computer model has a 256K cache. This means the microprocessor has 256K of memory to help speed it up.

What's the point? The larger the cache, the better the microprocessor will perform. Use the cache size for comparison when you get around to shopping.

✔ Quick Review

The microprocessor is the most important part of all your computer hardware, because it controls the rest of the computer. But more important than that are your software needs. You need to review the requirements for the software you selected to determine which microprocessor your computer should have.

For example, if your software claims it can use an 80386 or greater microprocessor, then you can select an 80386, 80486, or Pentium.

GREAT ADVICE ▸ Which one should you choose? Follow this advice: Select the latest, fastest microprocessor you can afford. Don't buy anything less than a 486, selecting a 386 microprocessor only if you can't afford anything else or you're buying some type of custom or laptop computer and nothing else is available. If you can afford a Pentium or compatible "586" chip, buy that. Then select the fastest speed.

When you've made your decision, write that ideal processor down on the worksheet at the front of this book. Make any additional notes on the worksheet as to your opinions as well.

Chapter 7

Memory (RAM)

Getting Enough Temporary Storage for Your Computer

The microprocessor may be the most important part of your computer, but it needs a place to store information. Just like the Hollywood starlet needs her closet full of shoes, or a handyman needs his shed full of tools (or the computer guy has the obligatory stack of magazines dating back to 1982), the microprocessor needs storage — both long-term and temporary — for it to work.

Temporary storage is your computer's memory, or *RAM*. That's where the microprocessor does most of its business, because the microprocessor itself is merely a calculator-like device and has little storage.

Long-term storage is provided by your computer's disk drives. Information "saved" on a disk is there almost forever, available until it's erased or overwritten — just like a cassette or video tape. (In fact, it's the same technology.)

In your computer, you need both temporary and long-term storage. That's not even an issue. What's important is for you to figure out how much of each type of storage you need. This chapter covers temporary storage; the next chapter deals with permanent storage.

Temporary Storage: Computer Memory (or RAM)

Random Access Memory (*RAM*) is where your computer's microprocessor temporarily stores information. The more memory your computer has, the more information the microprocessor can "play with," and therefore, the more your computer can do.

The amount of RAM in your computer depends on a number of things:

- How much memory your software requires
- How much memory your computer can hold
- How much memory you can afford

The idea is to have as much memory in your computer as you need without ever running short. This means your software can do the job it was meant to do, and you'll also have memory to spare or in anticipation of future programs that require even more memory.

> ### Random Access Memory, RAM, memory — what gives?
>
> Computer memory is technically called *Random Access Memory* and is commonly abbreviated *RAM*. You'll find this term on the sides of software boxes, on computer cartons, and generally all over. This book refers to computer memory as *memory*, since I personally believe acronyms to be the work of the devil.

> ### Why is there memory?
>
> Your computer's microprocessor chip is similar to the absent-minded professor — very forgetful. The microprocessor has very little memory of its own, aside from a tiny amount it uses. It needs some other place to store the instructions, data, and miscellaneous information that it isn't immediately using.

Measuring computer memory

In science fiction films of old, memory was measured by the "bank." Mr. Spock would mention that the memory banks were "fried," or some benevolent computer would claim that the evil scientist had erased all of its memory banks. (This would have meant the computer couldn't talk, but don't let accuracy stand in the way of plot!) There's actually some truth to the "bank" theory of measuring memory. But for real computers in the real world, the yardstick by which memory is measured is the *byte*.

A byte is a storage unit — like those rental storage garages where people put stuff they're too ashamed to admit they own and too proud to throw away. In a computer, bytes are used to store one character in memory, such as a letter of the alphabet or some other character.

The best way to picture a byte is to suppose that it is capable of storing one piece of Alpha-Bits™ cereal. The letter *A* is a byte. In a computer, you'd need one byte of memory to store the letter *A*. You'd need eleven bytes to store the word "bellybutton."

As you can imagine, you need a lot of memory (RAM or bytes) to write and store a memo with a word processor. Because of this, computer memory is measured in *Ks,* rather than individual bytes. 1K is equal to 1,024 bytes of memory. Again using the Alpha-Bits™ cereal example, 1K would be one bowl of cereal — without the milk.

Most computers have thousands of K of memory, millions in fact. When the first IBM PC was introduced in 1982, 64K of memory was common. By the mid-'80s, computers with ten times that amount, or 640K, were a must. That's 640 times 1,024, actually 655,360 bytes of RAM — a lot of cereal.

Today, computers have millions of bytes in them. *MB,* or just *M,* is used as an abbreviation for megabyte, or 1,024K, roughly 1 million bytes. (There's no need to bother with the actual number of bytes; suffice it to say, it's huge.) Or, to bring you back to the example, 1 megabyte is just about a three year's supply of Alpha-Bits™ cereal.

What's important here is that K (pronounced *kay*) is a *kilobyte*, or about one thousand characters of computer storage. MB (pronounced *em bee*) is a *megabyte*, or about 1 million characters of storage. When you see a software package claiming that it needs "3MB of RAM" to run, know that you need a computer with at least 3 megabytes of temporary memory.

Memory and your software

Knowing how many megabytes of memory your computer should have depends on your software's appetite. Here is where you need to be a little cautious; software developers are memory-shy when it comes to numbers (which you'll soon discover). If you see "2MB minimum, but 4MB recommended," it means you *need* 4MB — 4 megabytes or 4 million bytes of memory — for the software to run as well as it can.

If you've done your homework, then you should have a list of software and its memory requirements on the software worksheets at the front of this book. *Don't total the memory requirements!* Instead, find the largest number. For example, say some graphics package needs "4MB of RAM" to work. Everything else is less than that, so 4MB of memory is the amount of memory you'll want to have in your computer. (This doesn't mean you can't have more, or that you won't need more — it's just a starting point.)

But wait! You're not done. Knowing how much memory your software needs is only the first step. You also need to be sure that your computer can have that much memory available, installed into its belly.

Why is 1K equal to 1,024 bytes and not 1,000 bytes even?

What? Were you expecting logic from the computer industry? The truth is that things in a computer work around the number two — or *binary*. Two to the tenth power, or 2^{10}, equals 1,024. Computers like the number two, and 1,024 is the closest power of two to the number 1,000. So there.

> ### Bits and bytes
>
> Technically, the smallest storage unit in a computer is the *bit*. That's a contraction of the words *binary digit*, which is a scientific term for either a 1 or a 0. This works out because a bit is only capable of being "on" or "off" inside a computer. The computer believes "on" to be equal to the value 1 and "off" to be equal to 0.
>
> Bits can get unwieldy to deal with, so computer scientists corral them into groups of eight and call that group a *byte* — which is their attempt at being funny (bit-byte).

Knowing how much memory your computer can hold

Your software may want 4MB of memory, but can that amount be installed in your computer? There are two ways to find out.

First, each microprocessor is capable of using a given amount of memory. For some microprocessors, this is a limited amount. Other microprocessors, particularly the ones available today, can use a tremendous amount of memory — more than you would ever need or could afford.

The amount of memory your microprocessor is capable of using depends on its *bit width*. Rather than get into that here, refer to Table 6-1 in Chapter 6 to see how many megabytes the various PC processors can gobble up. This amount is the maximum memory you can install — provided you're crazy or rich enough — in your computer.

Second, a more practical limitation on how much memory can fit in your computer is how much memory you can physically plug into the computer's main circuitry board.

Computer memory comes on tiny chips that are grouped into rows of eight or nine called — get this — a *bank* of memory. (That's where memory bank comes in, from the old sci-fi movies.) Each PC is designed to hold only so many banks of memory and, therefore, is limited to a certain maximum. So even though you may buy a computer with a 486 microprocessor, and it theoretically could have 4,096MB of memory installed (see Table 6-1), there wouldn't physically be enough room for all that memory in your computer. Because of this, computer manufacturers only let you plug in a given amount of memory.

> ### Dealing with the bane of conventional, extended, and expanded memory
>
> Memory terms can drive you insane! Two examples are extended and expanded memory. They're different types of memory, but you think they could have used words that aren't so similar to describe them. Hopefully, the following will help:
>
> **Conventional Memory.** This is the basic 640K of memory in your computer, the first 640K. If you buy a computer with 1MB of memory, then you have 640K of it as conventional and 384K as extended memory.
>
> **Extended Memory.** This is any memory you have on your computer over 640K. So if you have a 4MB computer, you have 3MB — and change — of extended memory.
>
> **Expanded Memory.** This is a special type of memory used for DOS programs. It requires a special software program that creates the expanded memory using whatever extended memory your computer has. Fortunately, the special software program — a *memory manager* — takes care of the details without any fuss on your behalf.

Typically, a PC has room for about 32MB of memory total. Some models may have more, some less. You want to make sure that your computer can always have more memory installed, so watch out for some of the cheaper models that may be limited to only 4MB or 8MB of memory total. Always make sure that you can add more memory in the future, even though you may now think you'll never need it or can't afford it.

Buying enough memory

You buy memory when you buy your computer. But like selecting the color for your new refrigerator or the horsepower of your new riding lawnmower, the amount of memory you have installed is up to you. The salesperson will want to know whether you want 1MB, 2MB, 4MB, 8MB, or whatever in your computer. It's your choice, since it's your computer. And the more memory, the higher the cost.

CHAPTER 7: MEMORY (RAM)

GREAT ADVICE ▸ My advice: Buy as much memory as you can afford. At a minimum, try to put 4MB of memory in your computer. If you can't afford that much, then at least have 1MB or 2MB. If you can afford 8MB or even 16MB, you'll be well ahead of the game.

Memory inside your computer

Each computer is configured with a different amount of memory. Common quantities are 640K, 1MB, 2MB, 4MB, 8MB, 16MB, and up. If a computer advertises itself as coming with "0K RAM," it means you have to go out and buy the memory extra. Figure that in when comparing prices! All computers need memory.

Hurry up and wait state

A troublesome term you may encounter when dealing with computer memory is the *wait state*. This is a tiny tick of the microprocessor's heartbeat — a pause — when it must sit and wait for its memory to catch up with it. For example, you may see a PC with 1 wait state. Okay. So it has to wait awhile. However, you may see more zero wait states, which means the computer is just a nose faster. (The technical reasons behind wait states are rather baffling, so don't bother with them. Just remember that this is a speed issue.)

63

✔ Quick Review

Memory is where the action happens inside your computer. The microprocessor needs memory to think, and your software needs it to help you get your work done.

To figure out how much memory you need, refer back to Chapter 4 and to your software worksheets at the front of this book. Look over the list and find the software that requires the most total RAM. It should be a huge number, possibly 1MB, 2MB, or even higher. Write that number down on the proper line on the hardware worksheet at the front of this book. This is how much memory your new computer needs.

If you can afford more memory, by all means get more. For example, if your software only needs 3MB max, consider getting 4MB. If you can afford a PC with 8MB of memory, get it.

Chapter 8
Disk Drives

Getting Enough Permanent Storage for Your Computer

Why is memory (RAM) temporary storage? Because memory needs a constant flow of electricity to maintain its information. When the computer is switched on, memory is available and ready to store information. When the power is turned off, memory is off, and all the data stored there is lost — poof!

Obviously, what you do on the computer is important. You'll need a permanent place to store the stuff you do, a place that won't be subject to *poof!* every time you switch off your PC. That permanent storage is provided by your computer's disk drives, of which there are two main types: the hard drive and the floppy drive.

> ### The difference between megabytes in memory and megabytes on disk
>
> Your computer's temporary (memory) and permanent (disk) storage are both measured in bytes or, more accurately, megabytes. Some people find this confusing. For example, they may read on the side of the software that a program needs 2MB of RAM and 6.5MB of disk storage. Please keep in mind that these are two different things. The RAM value is memory, which the computer uses when working with the program. The disk storage value is storage space — like in a closet. Don't confuse the two values! A program may need more disk space than memory. If so, fine. In fact, it's very common. Don't think your memory and disk space values should match. That's just not the way it works. (As long as you follow the instructions offered in this book, everything will work out fine.)

The Hard Drive

Every computer needs a *hard disk drive*. This is true no matter what. In the olden days (maybe seven years ago), it was possible to use a computer without a hard drive. Not today.

Hard drives are attractive for three reasons:

- Speed
- Storage capacity
- Cost

Compared to floppy drives, hard disks are faster, capable of storing much more information, and relatively inexpensive for the amount of storage you get for your dollar.

> ### How disk drives work
>
> Disk drives are the most common device for storing computer programs and data. They work like a magnetic record player — only the record, in this case, is the disk. Floppy diskettes, for example, are made of essentially the same stuff as cassette tapes — except the floppy disk is smashed flat, like a pancake. The disk in a hard drive is rigid metal coated with a magnetic oxide, also flat like a pancake.
>
> Each disk drive has a *recording head,* like a cassette recorder. This recording head floats back and forth over the flat, magnetic surface of the diskette. Because the diskette spins 'round and 'round, the recording head can quickly locate any particular point anywhere on the disk. It can then read or write data from that specific point to or from the computer's memory.

Table 8-1	Other Names for Hard Disks
Other Name	*Explanation*
Hard drive	The hard disk and its drive or case
Hard disk	The hard disk itself (used interchangeably with hard drive)
Fixed disk	Early IBM term for a hard drive
Hard file	Present IBM term for a hard drive
Winchester disk	A nickname given to early IBM hard drives that could store 30MB on two disks, that is, 30/30, like the rifle

Hard disk speed

Hard disks, like almost everything else with computers, are measured in speed. Unlike the microprocessor, which is measured in megahertz, a hard drive's speed, called the *access time,* is measured in milliseconds. One millisecond is one thousandth of a second, and it's often abbreviated "ms."

The faster the hard disk, the smaller its access time value. And the smaller the access time value, the more quickly you can get at your data.

The millisecond rating for any hard disk you buy today should be less than 20 ms. Anything greater is considered "slow" (though the first PC hard drive had a speed of 65 ms, and up until a few years ago, a 40 ms rating was considered rather zippy). Speed ratings of 12 ms and below are considered typical, with any speed in the single digits absolute heaven.

This may sound silly since you're measuring speed here in milliseconds. I mean, how noticeable can ten milliseconds be? However, differences in hard disk speed are *very* noticeable — especially for the so-called "disk intensive" applications (data bases, mailing lists, and so on). Anytime you find yourself working on a faster or slower hard drive, you'll notice the speed difference right away.

GREAT ADVICE ▶ I recommend you avoid any hard drive that's slower than 20 ms (that is, has a speed value greater than 20). Try to stick to hard drives with a 16 to 12 ms access time. You'll find that larger hard drives have faster access times, so often it's best just to opt for size here and get the faster access time as a bonus.

Hard disk storage capacity

The average hard disk drive sold today can store about 200MB of data. This is the bare minimum you need for running today's hoggish programs. Hard drive sizes will vary, however; you can buy anything from a 40MB hard drive on up to 5GB — 5 *gigabytes,* or over 5,000MB!

There really is no rhyme or reason behind hard drive sizes. In fact, your first PC may have 210MB or 340MB or some other odd number. Don't let that faze you. As long as you don't buy a hard drive with too little storage space, you'll be okay.

GREAT ADVICE ▶ So which size hard drive should you get? Again, return to the software worksheets at the beginning of this book. The column that lists disk size shows how many megabytes of disk storage space your software desires. Add up those numbers! Then add another 40MB just for the heck of it. Finally, double the number.

For example, suppose your software requirements add up to 60MB of disk storage. Add 40MB and you get 100MB. Double that and you get 200MB, which is the typical hard drive size sold today. But if you get a larger number, you'll need to find a hard drive at least that size instead. Write that number down for the size of your hard drive in the hardware worksheet at the beginning of this book.

CHAPTER 8: DISK DRIVES

Hard disk cost: Cheap! Cheap! Cheap!

Another reason not to skimp on hard drive capacity is that they're cheap. The price of a hard drive is incredibly low when you're talking about how much storage you get per dollar, as measured by dollars-per-megabyte.

For example, suppose that you're going all out and getting a 500MB hard drive. It should cost you less than $200 for that drive. That works out to 40 cents per megabyte for storage. Cheap!

The larger the hard drive, the cheaper storage is. A 1GB hard drive will cost maybe 50 cents per megabyte. Smaller hard drives will be more expensive, but I haven't seen anything recently for more than 75 cents per megabyte.

This may not mean anything, but just ten years ago the price of storage was about $12.50 per megabyte. It declines a little bit every year; we're now down to the ludicrous 50 cents a megabyte — and falling!

The secret hard drive controller

Another hidden aspect of your hard drive is the *controller*. The controller is a special piece of electronics that plugs into your computer, connecting the hard drive mechanism to your computer and (eventually) to the microprocessor.

With IBM-style computers, you have a choice of which hard drive controller you want. Presently, two standards exist: the Integrated Drive Electronics, or *IDE*, and the Small Computer System Interface, or *SCSI*, which is endearingly pronounced "scuzzy." Both of these terms are used as acronyms, so you'll have to live with them.

IDE. IDE controllers are the most common and least expensive. These controllers handle a variety of disk drives quite easily, and their only real drawback is that they don't handle very large (upwards of 500MB) drives well. This is actually a limitation of DOS (and Windows). If you buy an IDE drive larger than 500MB, it must be divided up into smaller portions because DOS can't fathom an IDE drive larger than 500MB. This limitation may be mended by the time you read this.

SCSI. SCSI controllers are very versatile and handle not only a variety of hard drives but other devices as well. The full scoop on SCSI controllers is offered in the next chapter, should you wish to pursue them.

GREAT ADVICE My advice is to choose a controller based on two things: the size of your hard drive and whether or not you plan on running Windows.

If you need a hard drive larger than 500MB, then go with SCSI. Otherwise, IDE is fine. Also, if you plan on adding a CD-ROM, scanner, or other type of SCSI device to your computer, SCSI is a better bet.

If you're running Windows, then there is a minor speed penalty for going with SCSI. For some reason that I'm sure is way over my head, IDE hard drives work faster with Windows. However, you may still need a SCSI controller in your computer for other reasons. (More on this in the following chapter.)

The Floppy Drive

All computers should have at least one floppy drive. Even with a hard disk, at least one floppy disk drive is required for the transporting, backing up, and initial loading of programs and data onto the hard disk.

There are a few interesting issues surrounding floppy disks but nothing overly crucial. In fact, I can almost promise you that your computer will come with a floppy drive capable of eating diskettes that are $3^1/_2$ inches square and can hold 1.44MB of information. Still, there are a few issues about the drives worth bringing up.

Floppy disk sizes

Even though a floppy disk is round, its container is square — like pizza! A floppy disk is measured along the square edge to give you its relative size. Since the dawn of the personal computer, three sizes have become popular. First came the 8-inch floppy diskette, then the $5^1/_4$-inch "minifloppy." Eventually, the $5^1/_4$-inch disk became the most popular; it was dubbed the "floppy disk," and 8-inch disks were used as Frisbees by college students on graduation day.

Presently, the most popular disk size is the 3½-inch disk. (It was originally called the "microfloppy," but now it's just a "floppy disk" like the others were before they became obsolete.) See Figure 8-1 for examples of the 5¼-inch and 3½-inch floppy disks.

Not only does the smaller 3½-inch disk hold more information than its larger forebears, but it's durable. The disk is enclosed in a hard, plastic shell. It's very easy to slip into a shirt pocket or briefcase without it experiencing the dreaded "el-foldo" of the larger, floppier disks.

Figure 8-1: A 5¼-inch and a 3½-inch diskette.

Sides and densities

When floppy drives were first developed, they could read and write on only one side of a diskette. The quality of the diskette surface and the technology of the drives dictated that data would be recorded in a format now called *single density*. These drives and the diskettes used in them are referred to as single-sided/single-density, or *SS/SD*.

As the desire to squeeze more data onto the same diskette grew, and as disk technology improved, a single-sided/ double-density (*SS/DD*) format was developed. SS/DD squeezed twice as much data in the same space, thereby doubling the storage capacity of every diskette. However, information was still on only one side of the disk.

One day, some brilliant technician decided that, well heck, the bottom of the disk was made of the same material as was the top. So why not put a read/write head (as they are called) on the bottom of the disk drive so you can read and write to both sides of the disk? Thus, the double-sided drive was introduced.

The double-sided/double-density (*DS/DD*) drive sported two recording heads, allowing information to be written to and read from both sides of the diskette and increasing the storage space four times over the old SS/SD disk drives. A 5¼-inch, DS/DD disk holds 360K of programs and data; a 3½-inch DS/DD disk holds 720K of data. But the scientists didn't stop there. Oh, no!

Soon a new format was developed, along with a drive capable of eating those types of diskettes. This drive is called a *High Capacity* or *High Density* (HD) drive. The High Capacity drive can still read and write to the older DS/DD format diskettes, but its primary use is at the "high" level. A 5¼-inch, HD disk holds 1.2MB of information; a 3½-inch HD disk holds 1.44MB.

Presently, the 3½-inch, HD disk is the most popular type of disk found on just about every new PC sold. A newer format, Extended Density (ED), is also available, though not really that popular.

GREAT ADVICE Your computer should have at least one, 3½-inch, HD drive. Consider buying a second, 5¼-inch disk drive only if you'll be working with other people who have computers that only have that older format. Otherwise, you can kiss the 5¼-inch disk format good-bye.

Floppy disks must be formatted

To use a floppy diskette in your disk drive, the disk must first be *formatted*. This is because computer owners can go to the store and buy a 3½-inch diskette. They then use their computer's operating system to prepare that diskette for use. Because the store wants to sell floppy disks to everyone, the disks aren't generally pre-formatted.

Formatting disks is a task you'll do with your computer and your operating system once you set everything up. Just remember these few points when you purchase diskettes:

- Always buy the proper diskette size and capacity for your floppy drive.

- If you can find pre-formatted disks for your computer ("IBM formatted," for example), buy them. Otherwise, you must format the disks before you use them.
- Never attempt to "save money" by buying low-capacity diskettes and formatting them to a higher capacity.
- Likewise, don't format high-capacity diskettes to a lower capacity.

✔ Quick Review

All computers need at least one floppy drive and one hard drive for their long-term or permanent storage. The only issue at stake is how big a hard drive you need.

First, pick a hard drive controller. If you're going with a drive larger than 500MB, or if you also plan on buying a CD-ROM drive or any other SCSI *peripheral,* pick SCSI. Otherwise, an IDE drive will be perfect. Mark your selection on the worksheet at the beginning of this book.

Second, calculate the size of your hard drive based on the formula in this chapter: Take the sum total of the hard disk space requirements from all your software worksheets at the front of this book and total them. Then add 40MB for good measure. Take that total and double it. That's the size of the hard drive you need. Write that number down on the hardware worksheet at the front of this book.

For your floppy drive, you'll need at least one $3^1/_2$-inch, high density (HD) drive. Check that off on your hardware worksheet. And if you need any additional floppy drives, or require a $5^1/_4$-inch drive, check that off on your hardware worksheet as well.

Chapter 9
The Monitor and Keyboard

■ ■

Two Basic Items Attached to Your Computer

Without a monitor or keyboard, your computer would be deaf and mute. A computer is pretty worthless unless you can tell it what you want it to do. There also needs to be a way for the computer to report its results back to you.

The mouth, or face, of a computer system is its *monitor*. The computer communicates to you using its monitor, displaying information for you to read. The way *you* communicate to the computer is by using its keyboard — which acts like the computer's ears.

This chapter covers monitors and keyboards. Unlike computers of old, today's PCs generally have separate monitors and keyboards (they aren't built-in anymore). You have a choice! Knowing a few things about your future monitor or keyboard before you pick one out helps make communicating (and living) with your computer better in the long run.

The Monitor ("Look at Me! I'm as Pretty as a Trinitron TV!")

There are two ways a computer can communicate with you: through its printer (covered in Chapter 11) or its monitor. Though printing is necessary and an important part of what your computer does, the best way for a computer to communicate with you is with its video display, or monitor. No personal computer is complete without one.

For nearly all computers, the monitor is an add-on. The main part of the computer consists of the microprocessor, memory, the disk drives, and other stuff "inside the box." Although some kinds of computers offer a specific same-label monitor, it's still possible to pick and choose from a wide variety of monitors for your own computer needs.

Looking good

A monitor on a PC has two different parts. The first part is the monitor itself — the TV set-like thing that sits on top or alongside your computer box. The second part is hidden inside your computer. It's the monitor's *graphics controller* card, also known as a *video board* or *graphics adapter*. That's the circuitry required to run the monitor, and it plays an important role in the quality and quantity of the colors and graphics you'll see on-screen.

Selecting the proper graphics card

Great Advice ▶ When it comes to your computer's monitor, you should select your graphics card first. That is, shop for the circuitry to control the monitor, and then buy a monitor that's compatible with (designed to work well with) that graphics card. This way you'll get the best graphics for your computer without being limited by your monitor. It helps if you remember that the controller controls the monitor — like a driver controls a car — and not the other way around.

There are four standard PC video graphics cards that exist today. They're all acronyms and they're all pronounced with the letters (or numbers) only:

- VGA
- SVGA
- 8514/a
- XGA

You can look up what the acronyms mean in this book's glossary if you're curious. Essentially, these alphabet-soup letter combinations describe PC graphics cards with different degrees of sophistication. This is measured by the number of colors the card can display and the graphics resolution, which describes how detailed the graphics can be.

GREAT ADVICE ▶ My advice is to buy an SVGA or better (8514/a or XGA) graphics card. By itself, the SVGA standard will suit you fine. If you have more money to spend, buy a 2MB SVGA card (a graphics card with 2 megabytes of video memory). And if you're a graphics artist, you can opt for an even better card. But no matter what, make sure that it's compatible with the SVGA standard.

Working out the graphics resolution

Resolution refers to how many dots (called *pixels*) a graphics card can display on the screen, typically shown as horizontal and vertical values. For example, a resolution of "640 x 400" means there are 640 dots marching across the screen (horizontal) and 400 dots marching down (vertical), for a total of 256,000 dots on the screen. A lower resolution would be 320 x 200 (half of the previous value). Higher resolutions would have larger values. And the higher the resolution, the finer and less "jaggy" the image.

Buying enough video memory

Video memory is special memory (RAM) used to help your PC's graphics controller display lots of colors and high graphics resolution. The more video memory you have, the better your graphics card — and the more expensive.

Typically, you'll find SVGA cards with 1MB (1 megabyte) of video memory. That's fine for most of us. Two megabytes are good for graphics artists and those who can afford it.

Beware of video cards with zero video memory! You need video memory, and installing it "later" shouldn't be an option. Buy your video memory when you buy the card.

77

Picking out a monitor

Once you've selected your video card, plucking out a matching monitor is a snap. Sure, there are lots of technical things about matching "monitor frequency" to "card frequency." But if you tell the salesperson about your video card, you can get a monitor to match with no technological complications.

Right away you should know that you don't have to buy your monitor from the same manufacturer as your computer. Most people do, and they're usually happy. But if you can find something better or more economical, you can always "hold the monitor" — just like you'd hold the mayo at a deli — and buy it separately.

Here are a few things to look for in a monitor:

- Size (diagonally)
- Dot pitch
- Interlacing
- Frequency

Size. The diagonal size of your monitor is about the most key issue. Typical computer monitors measure 14 inches to 17 inches diagonally (from the upper-left corner to the lower-right). Larger monitors are available if you want that Big Screen look, or if your eyes require more screen to see what you're doing.

Dot pitch. The *dot pitch* refers to the distance between the tiny dots that make up the image on your monitor's screen. The smaller the dot pitch, the finer the image the monitor can display. Typical dot pitch values are .41mm (millimeters) on down to .25 and lower. The smaller the value, the better (and more expensive).

Interlacing. *Interlacing* refers to the way the monitor displays information on-screen. Older, cheaper monitors and all TV sets are *interlaced*. That means the electron gun inside the monitor makes two swipes across the screen to paint one image. This tends to cause the screen to flicker. Computer monitors that use a *non-interlaced* (NI) method don't flicker as much and are easier on the eyes. You want a non-interlaced monitor.

Frequency. Finally, there is the monitor's frequency and a bunch of other technical attributes that only computer scientists love to banter about. Basically, your monitor's frequency should match (or be able to match) that of your graphics card. If you've followed the steps outlined in this chapter, that won't be a problem.

> **GREAT ADVICE** The best way to find a good monitor is to go to a computer store and *look* at them. Technical specifications are one thing, but actually seeing how a monitor looks is best. For example, I thought this one monitor was technically superior, but it looked too "blue" to me. So I bought a monitor that displayed crisper reds.

When comparing monitors, it helps if they're both displaying the same image. You should set the brightness and contrast knobs both to the "center" position. Don't let the salesperson adjust the knobs; you want to verify that you're seeing a fair comparison yourself.

79

Keyboards

Keyboards, like monitors, come in a variety of types and styles. It can almost be said that no two keyboards are exactly alike. Fortunately, they're all similar enough that you can find one you like without it being too much of an oddball.

Before personal computers became popular, computer terminals had these incredible keyboards. They started with the basic keyboard layout found on a typewriter. Then they added a number of very specific function keys. Some terminals had keys that actually said INSERT LINE, MOVE BLOCK, CLOSE FILE, and GET ME CHIPS. These days, computer keyboards are a little more conservative.

Hunt 'n peck

As with choosing a monitor, some computers come with their own keyboard, or you can choose a specialty keyboard. Gone are the days when computers came with an attached keyboard (or the keyboard was actually part of "the computer"). With today's computers, you have a choice.

The typical computer keyboard, standard with just about every computer sold today, is called the 101-key "Enhanced" keyboard (see Figure 9-1). It really does have 101 keys on it, the extras scattered about the standard typewriter keys like so many weeds in a garden.

Figure 9-1: The 101-key "Enhanced" keyboard.

There is very little deviation from this standard keyboard layout. Some computer makers put their names on the keyboards. Sometimes you see lights on various keys (Caps Lock, Num Lock, and so on). And each keyboard has a different touch and feel. These are all minor considerations that don't really affect how the keyboard is used. But if you want to get unique and funky, you're allowed that as well.

Extremely funky keyboards

Choosing a keyboard isn't as fussy a thing as picking out a monitor. For me it is. I like a keyboard with sharp, responsive keys. Mushy keyboards are the bane of any good typist. But beyond the basics, most keyboards don't have much to offer . . . unless you go hunting for the funky keyboards!

Since all computer manufacturers settled on the 101-key keyboard a while back, there has been little deviation from the standard keyboard layout. You will find, however, some keyboards with a few extras in them or on them just to be different.

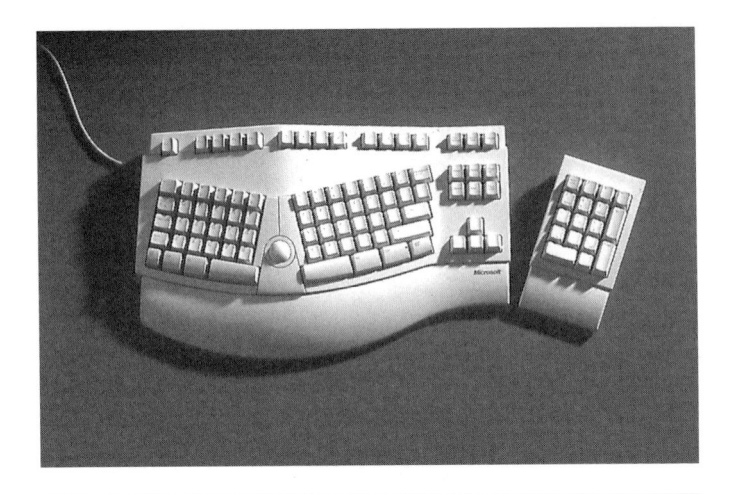

Figure 9-2: An ergonomic keyboard.

The most popular deviation is the *ergonomic* keyboard. This is a keyboard that has a funky shape, primarily designed to be easy on your wrists. An example is the new Microsoft keyboard, shown in Figure 9-2. Other keyboards have similar shapes, including one I've seen that looks like it's broken in the middle, with each half of the keyboard turned up like the sides of a mountain.

Aside from ergonomic variations, some keyboards come with special features. The most popular feature is the built-in computer mouse or "thumb ball" for controlling a mouse pointer on-screen. I've seen keyboards with built-in calculators, clocks, and even stereo speakers.

All this bonus, funky stuff costs more money, of course. If you feel your wrists could benefit from an ergonomic keyboard, look into one. Or if you opt for a funky keyboard, look into that as well. See what your dealer has to offer. Some places let you substitute keyboards; find out before you buy.

✔ Quick Review

The monitor is the computer's face and mouth, and the keyboard is the computer's ear. You need both if you want to communicate with your computer, and you need to pick something you like if you want it to be a pleasant experience.

Before selecting a monitor, first choose a graphics card or graphics adapter. This is the circuitry that sits inside your computer and controls the monitor. Select a card compatible with the SVGA (or Super VGA) standard with at least 1MB of video memory. As usual, buy a more expensive standard or more video memory if your software requires it or if it's in your budget. Write this information down on the hardware worksheet at the front of this book.

Select a monitor based on your graphics card selection. Go to the store and view various monitors if you can; otherwise, pick one based on its compatibility with your graphics card, its size, and other technical miscellany. Write that information down on your hardware worksheet when you're done.

Finally, pick out a keyboard. If this seems puzzling to you, just select the 101-key Enhanced keyboard that everyone else uses. Otherwise, you can research keyboards further if you feel a funky model or something more to your personal needs is required. Jot down anything special about your keyboard on your hardware worksheet.

Chapter 10
Ports, Mouses, and Other Stuff

Completing Your Basic Hardware

Monitors and keyboards are the primary, and most obvious, ways for a computer and its user to communicate. Another way the computer communicates is with *ports*. This communication isn't the computer-to-human type. Instead, the computer uses ports to communicate with the outside world, other computers, and certain devices such as printers and, believe it or not, mice.

This part of your computer hardware journey covers ports. Non-technically speaking, a port is a "hole" in the back of the computer. Anything that plugs into the computer that isn't the keyboard, monitor, or power cable probably plugs into a port.

Ports

There are two popular types of ports on most computers: serial and printer. Other ports include mouse ports for connecting mice and other "pointing devices"; Analog-to-Digital (A-to-D) ports, used for scientific applications such as connecting joysticks to your computer, or MIDI devices for connecting musical instruments; and SCSI — "scuzzy" — ports that can hook up to a variety of devices, such as hard disks, CD-ROM drives, scanners, and so on.

Table 10-1 lists most of the common ports found on a PC, for your referencing pleasure. But keep in mind that the two most popular are the serial and printer ports.

Table 10-1 Types of Ports Your PC Can Sport

Port	Other Names	Connects Your Computer to . . .
Printer	Parallel, ECP/EPP, Centronics	A printer, mostly (sometimes networks, hard drives, other devices)
Serial	Modem, RS-232	A modem, mouse, other PC, and so on
Mouse	InPort	A mouse
Joystick	A-to-D	A joystick, scientific instruments, MIDI box for musical instruments
SCSI	"scuzzy"	A hard drive, CD-ROM, scanner, and so on

Your computer should come with at least one printer and one serial port. This is a must. You need the printer port to connect your computer to a printer. The serial port connects to a variety of devices, most of which you probably don't own now, but it helps to have at least one or two of them as well.

Printer ports

Shockingly enough, a printer port is the hole in the back of your computer where you'll plug your printer. Sometimes this hole is labeled "Printer," and sometimes it's given some other name, typically *Parallel port*. Recent model PCs may even have a picture of a wee li'l printer above this port (see Figure 10-1).

Figure 10-1: Here is a typical printer port on the back of some computer.

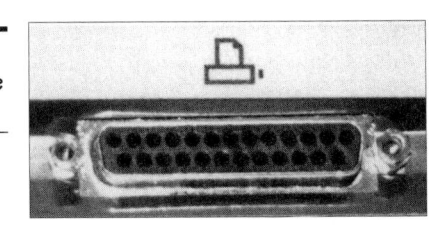

> ### What's a "parallel" port?
>
> A parallel port is the same thing as a printer port. Some compu-jockeys might also call it a *Centronics* port. Whatever, it's the hole into which you plug your printer's cable. The characters you send from the computer go out this port and to the printer.

Printer ports are also known as *parallel* ports. This term describes the way your computer sends each character to the printer; parallel ports work by sending each character to the printer eight bits at a time (each character, or byte, is composed of eight bits). The bits all travel side by side, as in a parade, each bit traveling down its own wire. It's called "parallel" because everything moves side by side.

GREAT ADVICE All computers need at least one printer port, which allows a printer to be hooked up to your PC. Today's computers typically come with one or two printer ports built-in. Some older or cheaper models may require you to buy a printer port as an add-on. Whatever. Make sure that your computer has at least one.

Serial ports

Printer ports are rather limited. They serve as a mode for one-way communication and primarily deal with the computer's printer. For two-way communication, serial ports are preferred.

> ### Look! Up in the sky! It's Super Parallel Port!
>
> Some manufacturers are making waves about a newer, faster printer port, dubbed the ECP/EPP port. This port is basically a super printer port, designed for fast, two-way communication with devices other than a printer. For example, you could hook up a network, hard drive, or some other interesting device to the ECP/EPP port. The acronym stands for Enhanced Capabilities Port/Enhanced Parallel Port, in case you have a burning desire to know such things.

Serial ports are often referred to as RS-232 or some other RS-numbered port. This is not a Radio Shack part number. Rather, "RS" stands for "Recommended Standard," and "232" is the number of the standard. (I suppose it was the 232nd standard the engineers could come up with that year.) But no matter what the compu-jockeys call it, it's a serial port.

Serial ports work by sending each character out of the computer one bit at a time. The serial port disassembles each character and squirts that character's bits out through the port. All the information travels in single file, as opposed to bits traveling eight abreast with a printer port. The serial port can also receive bits from another device, making it well-suited for two-way communication.

A variety of devices take advantage of the serial port and its capability for two-way communication. For example, you can use the serial port to connect two computers together. As long as both have serial ports, even two computers with different brand names can exchange information (provided they have the proper software, of course).

Modems plug into the serial port, which is why it's also called a modem port in some circles. A modem allows your computer to exchange information with other computers by using the phone system. (See Chapter 12 for more information on modems.)

Other devices you can hook up to a serial port include printers, mice, graphics tablets, digitizers, plotters, scanners, remote control devices, sensors and other scientific devices, and just about any of a dozen other unique and interesting items, most of which I can't think of right now.

Your computer should have at least one serial port, preferably two. Often this is the case with any new computer; it'll have two serial ports built right into the box (see Figure 10-2). You can always add more, but you'll probably be just fine with two.

Figure 10-2: A serial port on the back of some PC.

Mouse ports

A mouse port is not where Fievel Mousekewitz and his family first entered America. No, it's really a hole in the back of your computer where you'll plug a computer mouse or "pointing device."

Mouse ports are fairly common on today's computers. They're little round holes, similar to the things the keyboard plugs into on some PC models (see Figure 10-3). In fact, on some computers the keyboard and mouse ports are interchangeable.

Figure 10-3: A special mouse port.

On some older computer models, you could purchase a separate mouse expansion. On that card was a special mouse port, called the *InPort* by Microsoft. This was just another hole into which you'd plug your PC's mouse.

Finally, there is such a thing as a *serial mouse*. This isn't a psycho mouse that mentally torments cockroaches. It's just a mouse that can plug into one of your PC's serial ports (which is another reason why the serial port is so versatile).

Most of today's computer software can use a mouse to help move around a mouse "pointer" on-screen. If your software is among that group, you'll need a mouse as well as a mouse port to plug your mouse into. Refer to the section, "Mouses and Other Non-Furry 'Pointing Devices,'" later in this chapter for more information.

Joystick ports

A joystick port is simply a hole into which you'll plug your computer's joystick. It's also called an *Analog-to-Digital* port and can be used for other devices as well. For example, I have one of those twirly wind things (an anemometer) that's a home-brew weather kit. It sits on the roof of my office and plugs into my PC's joystick port.

Most PCs don't come with a joystick port. You must add it after the purchase by plugging a special expansion card into your system. If you're in luck, you may find that a joystick port comes standard with your PC's sound expansion card. (Sound and games go together well, though I'm not accusing you of wanting a joystick port for playing games. No way!)

MIDI ports

MIDI stands for Musical Instrument Digital Interface. It's a big, round ugly hole (hey — a port!) that you may have seen on any electronic musical instruments you may have lying around the house. The MIDI port is used to connect those instruments to each other and then to a computer. With the proper software, the computer can play the instruments, and lo, you'll have a symphony on your hands!

MIDI ports are basically the same thing as joystick ports (which should be called the A-to-D port in this instance). You plug a MIDI "box" into the joystick port, and then you plug the MIDI cables from your musical instruments into the MIDI box.

You also need special MIDI software to control the MIDI port and all the musical instruments. This stuff is really sophisticated. In fact, I've seen one program that "records" anything you play on a synthesizer and writes the music as you play it. It also works the other way, where you write music on the computer and it plays the various musical instruments as you dictate. (This is one of those fascinating things that computers can do that most people never suspect.)

SCSI ports

A SCSI port is a neat computer device, primarily pronounced "scuzzy." It stands for Small Computer System Interface and it's basically a very fast and versatile type of serial port.

SCSI ports are becoming more and more popular because there are a variety of devices that can be hooked up to them. The most common SCSI devices are hard drives. In fact, if you want a really huge hard drive (something 500MB in size or greater), you should get a SCSI controller and buy SCSI hard drives for it. But hard drives are not the limit of what a SCSI port can have plugged into it.

CHAPTER 10: PORTS, MOUSES, AND OTHER STUFF

> ### SCSI or SCSI/2
>
> You may occasionally stumble over the term SCSI/2 or SCSI2. Yes, this is the same "scuzzy" port that doesn't have a /2 in its name. It's just a little bit better. The /2 means "new and improved" in the computer business (it doesn't mean "one half"). Most of the SCSI stuff you buy today will be SCSI/2.

Because of the SCSI port's versatility, you can "daisy chain" SCSI devices. That means you can hook up your computer to more than one hard disk by simply plugging your first hard disk into a second — all via the one SCSI port. You could even add a SCSI scanner, optical disk, tape backup system, CD/ROM — all on the same line coming from one SCSI port. Because the SCSI port is faster than other ports, it can keep up with all the information sent between these devices and your computer.

GREAT ADVICE ▸ SCSI ports must be added to your computer. Presently, I know of no computer that comes with SCSI built-in (other than the Macintosh). If your overall PC design includes a CD-ROM drive or scanner in addition to the basic system, then get a SCSI port installed in your PC and go with the SCSI type of hard drive. That way you'll be ready for later expansion when the time comes.

Mouses and Other Non-Furry "Pointing Devices"

A *mouse* is an input device, like your keyboard. It controls a small arrow (also called the *mouse pointer* or *cursor*) on your computer screen. As you move the mouse around on your desktop, the small arrow moves around on-screen, mimicking the mouse's movements. Using the mouse, you can draw, select items, point and click the mouse's button(s) — all kinds of stuff. Many users find using a mouse easier and more intuitive than using arrow keys on a keyboard.

The mouse connects to your computer by either plugging into its own port (supplied as an expansion option on earlier computers) or by plugging into a serial port. If given a choice, buy the first type of mouse, also called the "bus mouse," which is a mouse that plugs into its own, special mouse port. There are just too many potential problems with a serial mouse to make it recommendable (unless your computer lacks an expansion slot for the bus mouse).

GREAT ADVICE The standard of all PC computer mouses is the Microsoft mouse. Microsoft may not have dreamt up the computer mouse, but it was first to come out with one for the PC. Because of that, you should get a mouse that's Microsoft-compatible.

Another major league mouse player (and I'm not talking Disney here) is Logitech. It makes more computer mouses than Microsoft — different shapes and styles, too. So either a Logitech or Microsoft mouse will do you fine. Or go with something more personal if you feel like it, always ensuring that your mouse is either Microsoft- or Logitech-compatible.

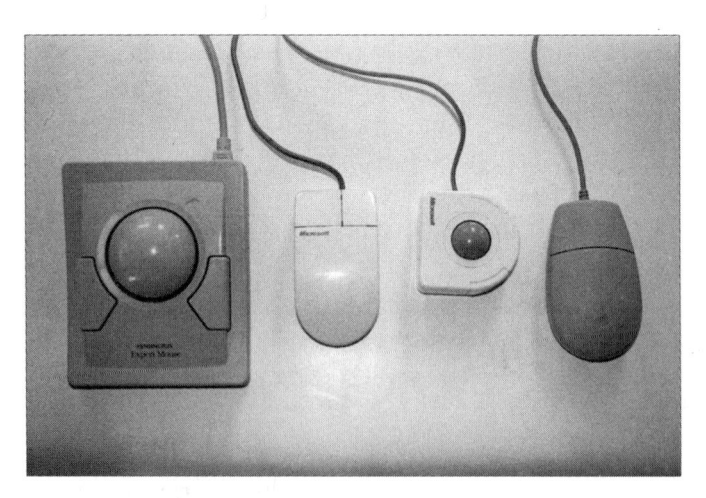

Figure 10-4: Different types of PC mouses.

CHAPTER 10: PORTS, MOUSES, AND OTHER STUFF

> ### Types of computer mouses
>
> There are three common variations on the computer mouse. There's the traditional mouse, the trackball mouse, and the funky mouse.
>
> The traditional mouse is a palm-sized device with one or more "buttons" and a cable trailing up and into the computer. The number of buttons can vary from one to three, with two being typical. (I've seen a 28-button mouse.) The cable is also optional since there are "infrared" mice that communicate with the PC using telepathy and other magic. Oh, and there are right-handed and left-handed mice, and they come in a variety of shapes and styles.
>
> Trackballs are very non-mouse-like (see Figure 10-4). They have a large, easily manipulated ball but they don't roll around on your desktop. This type of mouse (or "pointing device") is loved by artists and graphical types, but some users really hate them. Try one out before you buy.
>
> Funky mice consist of any mouse that isn't in the traditional or trackball style, such as a mouse shaped like a pen or "stylus." There are also tiny, joystick-like mice and pointing devices that use a touch-sensitive pad to move the cursor on-screen. Some laptops use a special key on the keyboard or a tiny stick or wand between two keys to move the cursor. It's a strange world.

Catching the Right Bus

One of the reasons the IBM PC became such a popular computer is due to its *open architecture*. This means that the computer can be expanded. It's possible to open up your PC's case and find *expansion slots*. Into those slots you plug bonus goodies called *expansion cards*. These cards allow you to customize and expand your computer beyond what the manufacturer set up.

There are lots of expansion cards available for the PC. In the old days, you added a printer or serial port using an expansion card. Today, those items are built-in. However, you may still need an expansion card for your PC's graphics, your hard drive, a SCSI expansion card, an internal modem, a sound card, or any number of interesting devices.

This all sounds wonderful — and it really is. But there is one tiny problem: Computer scientists absolutely hate the PC's expansion slots. Or, to be technical, they hate the PC's *bus,* which is the technical term for the expansion slots and how they communicate with the computer's microprocessor.

Different busses to catch

The problem with the PC's expansion slots, or bus, isn't yours to worry about. As long as you know which type of bus sits in your PC and you buy cards that plug into it, you're going to be fine.

To be academic, Table 10-2 lists the types of busses found in today's PCs. Odds are real good your system will have one or two of these types of busses for plugging in expansion slots.

GREAT ADVICE As far as recommendations go, keep with the ISA bus for now; don't bother with the EISA or MCA bus computers. Even though the ISA is an ancient standard (in computer terms), nearly all of the expansion cards you'll find in the store are of that type.

Table 10-2   Types of Busses in a PC

Bus Type	Comments
ISA	Most popular type of expansion slot in a PC. This bus can take both 8-bit (older) and 16-bit (newer) expansion cards.
EISA	Designed to expand upon and remove the weaknesses of the old ISA standard. You can plug ISA cards into an EISA bus, but it works best with its own (expensive) EISA cards.
MCA	Designed by IBM to supplant the old ISA bus, this one never caught on. Only certain PS/2 models support this one. These expansion cards are rare and not cheap.

The local bus is the express bus

Your computer may also come with a *local bus* type of expansion slot, which will probably be used for your system's video or hard drive or both. This is in addition to the ISA type of bus (which will handle most expansion slots). So, for example, you may buy a PC with ISA slots but with two or three special local bus slots for a fast video or fast hard drive expansion card.

Presently, there are two types of local bus expansion slots: VESA, or the VL-bus, and PCI. You can look in the glossary if you care about what they stand for (and it doesn't make understanding how they work any better). Either local bus will do you fine, though I've seen more PCI bus computers than VL-bus and would recommend them.

Why the local bus? Speed. The local bus has a very large "pipe" through which it can yell directly at the microprocessor. Two areas that can always use speeding up in a computer are the hard drive and graphics, which is why you'll see a lot of local bus hard drive and video cards. My advice is to go with a local bus if you possibly can.

✔ Quick Review

There is a lot to the world of ports in a PC. You're going to need at least one printer port for your printer, plus two serial ports just to be safe. If you need any more (that is, your software desires it), be sure to make a note of it on the hardware worksheet at the front of this book.

If you need a joystick for your computer, or if you need a special MIDI port, SCSI port, or any other type of port discussed in this chapter, jot it down on the worksheet as well. (You may already have done so if you've selected a SCSI hard drive.) Also, check your software worksheets from the front of the book to see whether you need a joystick port (for *whatever* reason). Remember that MIDI ports and joystick ports are the same thing. Also, if you plan on buying a sound card, it typically will come with a joystick/MIDI port.

Finally, you need to pick a mouse. If you don't know which type, you can save your decision for later. In the meantime, make a note of what you like on the hardware worksheet. You can save picking out a mouse for when you go shopping, or if you find a cute one with your name on it in an ad somewhere.

Chapter 11

All About Printers

Making Your Computer System Complete

Every computer needs a *printer*. Printers are responsible for what's called *hard copy*. Computers store information internally in memory or on disk as electronic bits of information. The hard copy is that same information printed so you can read or view it on paper.

With a printer, you get a physical recording, something you can touch, a letter you can mail, a list of names and addresses, some statistical projections you can show the big cheese at your office. Hard copy.

This chapter covers printers in depth. Next to the computer system itself, choosing the right printer is one of the tougher decisions. Because choosing a printer is important to completing your computer system, there's a lot of ground to cover. The more you know about it, the better prepared you'll be.

Yes, There Is a Vast Selection

Like computers and monitors, there are a lot of printers to choose from. Unlike computers and monitors, if you buy one brand of computer, you aren't "married" to a specific type of printer. There are dozens and dozens of printers on the market, and virtually all of them will work with your equipment.

The only crucial part is the connection between computer and printer. As mentioned in the preceding chapter, the majority of printers use a printer, or parallel, port. As long as your computer sports that type of hole, you can use it with any printer.

97

Different printers for different printing

There are several major kinds of computer printers: dot matrix, ink jet, thermal, daisy wheel, and laser printers. The most popular type — the one you want — is a laser printer. If you can't afford that, then dot matrix printers do a fine job. Ink jets and thermal printers are for special uses, and the daisy wheel printer is more of an anachronism than anything else.

All printers, no matter what the type, will get the printing job done. But because of the large selection, making a decision can be rough. There are many considerations involved with choosing a printer, and about the most important of these is price.

Table 11-1   Types of Computer Printers

Printer Type	Price Range	Comments
Dot Matrix	$150 - $400 U.S.	Good, general-purpose printers. You'll pay more for faster models. Color models are very expensive.
Ink Jet	$300 - $600+ U.S.	Typically color printers. You may pay more for "real good" quality.
Thermal	$250 - $550 U.S.	Portable printers used primarily with laptops. Prints only on flimsy, wax paper.
Daisy Wheel	-	Antiques I wouldn't pay $25 for.
Laser Printer	$550 - $2000+ U.S.	Fastest type of printer. Color models are more expensive.

How much?

The price of computer printers drops drastically but only every few years or so. In the summer of 1983, I paid $800 for my first printer. Before then, printers were considered expensive luxuries for personal computers; the printer was often purchased months after the computer, when users saved enough for the "superfluous" device that cost over $1,000.

Printer prices dropped again several years later, with a typical low-end cost of about $400. Then along came laser printers, costing about $5,000 each. I remember paying $4,000 for my first laser printer in 1988. The price finally fell below $2,000 a few years later, and today, you can pick up a nice laser printer for around $1,000. Dot matrix printers — better models than the one I bought for $800 — can be had for under $200. So this is really a major part of your computer expense. (In fact, the last computer I bought cost almost the same as its laser printer!)

The whole cycle is now repeating again with color laser printers (like a color photocopier). They're presently about $6,000 a piece, though soon the price will come crashing down to where most businesses and a few people in the upper tax brackets can afford them.

Printers do not come with cables!

Before diving into the fast and exciting world of printer types, it's important to note one little-known axiom of the computer-buying world: Printers do not come with cables.

Unlike a stereo or VCR, which comes with all the required cables, a computer printer doesn't come with everything you need to hook it up to your computer. The reason is that although all printer ports function the same, they aren't all shaped the same. For each computer, a specific cable exists. This doesn't mean your Gateway 2000 computer can't use a Dell computer cable, but it does mean that you must buy the cable extra. Expect to pay $5 to $15 for one, if it's not included with the printer (which it probably won't be).

> ### Printers don't come with paper, either
>
> It almost goes without saying that your printer will need paper. Though most printers will eat regular bond paper, you should get a ream or so of fanfold paper (this is the kind with the sheets connected to each other). The paper has little holes on the sides (called "tractor food") that help guide the paper through the printer. The tractor food is perforated so it can be removed after printing to make the paper normal size.
>
> Laser printers require no special paper, though buying "photocopier" or "Xerographic" paper is best. Avoid fancy paper that uses talc — that gritty dust — which can clog the laser printer's very expensive internal mechanisms.

Dot Matrix Printers

The most common type of computer printer is of the *dot matrix* variety. These are reliable, inexpensive, and robust devices for getting that all-important hard copy. Economical dot matrix printers are ideal for the home, and upper-end models can suit most business needs.

Dot matrix printers work by firing a series of pins, arranged vertically in a column. These pins stab at the printer's ribbon, forming a dot on the paper. As the print head (the device that contains the pins) moves back and forth, the pins create a pattern, a matrix of dots, in which characters are formed.

If you've ever seen the classic "computer printout," you've probably noticed the funny looking characters composed of tiny dots. This can be especially aggravating to read if the printer's ribbon has faded. However, with some printers and a good ribbon, dot matrix printouts are now considered acceptable as business correspondence. (Frankly, anything is better than my handwriting.)

The price of a dot matrix printer varies, depending on three factors: quality, speed, and carriage width.

Quality

The highest quality dot matrix printer is referred to as "near letter quality," or *NLQ*. Letter quality printers print like typewriters, producing very readable, clean, "un-dot-like" characters on a page. Near letter quality is the best a dot matrix printer can produce — as near to letter quality as it can get.

Good quality printers also produce what are called "true descenders" on their characters. For example, take the word *Egypt*. It has three characters with descenders: *g, y,* and *p*. On this page, the lower part of those characters drops below the baseline of the other characters on the line. These are called "true descenders." Some low-quality dot matrix printers fake descenders by shifting lowercase *g, y, p,* and *q* up a notch on the line.

Whether a printer can easily produce NLQ depends on how many pins are in its print head. A low-end dot matrix printer has only nine pins in its print head. Better models have 24 (see Figure 11-1). The 24-pin printers, because of the finer dot matrix, are more adept at producing NLQ characters. They are also more expensive.

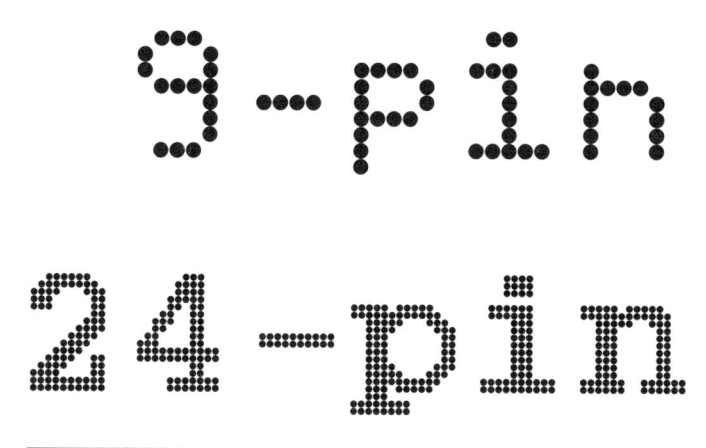

Figure 11-1: The differing output from a 9-pin and 24-pin printer.

Speed

The second pricing factor is the speed of the printer. The speed of a dot matrix printer is measured in characters per second, or *CPS*. The average printer moves along at about 180 to 200 CPS. Faster printers zip along at 360 CPS — but again, at a price.

Incidentally, these ratings should be used for comparison purposes only. (Your mileage may vary; city printing will be lower.) Printer companies are going to advertise printers at their fastest speed. To do this, they run the CPS tests under laboratory conditions, which produce better results than you'll get at home or in the office.

Fortunately, as far as the buyer is concerned, the CPS numbers are very good for comparison purposes. A 360 CPS printer is not always going to scream along at 360 characters per second. However, it's a good bet that printer will be twice as fast as a model advertised at 180 CPS.

Carriage width

Carriage width is the final determination of a dot matrix printer's price. There are two widths: standard and wide. The standard width accepts paper no bigger than the standard sheet size, $8^1/_2$ x 11 inches. Wide carriage printers cost a bit more and can accept paper up to 14 inches wide. These printers are ideal for businesses where printing forecasts and wide spreadsheets are a must.

Standard-width printers are also referred to as 80-column printers. Eighty columns is the number of pica pitch characters that can fit on one line of the page. The wide carriage printers print 132 pica characters on one line of the page.

It eats paper

One more thing! Dot matrix printers generally do not come with a paper-feeding mechanism. This is the device that guides the paper through the printer. There are three types of paper-feeding mechanisms: friction feed, tractor feed, and pin feed.

Friction feed is the same kind of paper-feeding mechanism used in typewriters. The paper is pinched between rollers, holding it steady while it's pressed through the printer. Friction feed is generally good for printing one sheet at a time, such as a business letterhead.

A tractor-feed mechanism sits above, or on top of, the printer and consists mainly of two sprocket wheels. These wheels have tiny bumps, or pegs, on them. The pegs fit in those tiny holes on either side of the computer paper and serve to both pull the paper through the printer and guide the paper so that it doesn't slip off to one side.

A pin-feed mechanism works on the same principle as a tractor feed. It too contains sprocket wheels that have pins to guide the paper through the printer. The only difference is that a pin-feeding mechanism sits behind the printer and actually pushes the paper through. Because of this, the paper stands a better chance of jamming than when a tractor feed is used.

Ink Jet and Color Printers

Ink jet printers work a lot like dot matrix printers. Instead of a metal pin forming a dot on the page, though, ink jet printers have tiny spray nozzles. A ball of ink is actually squirted (or, more accurately, lobbed) onto the paper. Because the ink is put directly on the paper, these printers require no ribbons. And since there is no mechanical movement involved, these printers are very quiet. Sometimes the brand name implies something about the printer's silence: Quietwriter, Whisperwriter, and so on. (Why don't some names deal with the "jet" aspect of the printer? Imagine: SquirtFast, SpitWriter, and InkZitter.)

Ink jet printers keep their ink in a reservoir instead of on a ribbon. Some brands actually have a number of reservoirs, each with a different color. The colors can be chosen via software to allow the printer to print in a rainbow of colors. More vividly, the printer can *dump* a full-color graphics image from a computer screen to paper — and do it all very quietly. I personally find this really neat-o.

Ink jet printers tend to be a little more pricey than their dot matrix cousins, and though they never really caught on in the mainstream of computing, they're very popular with laptops because they can be tiny and run off batteries. Nothing, however, beats the color graphics of these stealthy printers. Seeing a demo may make your eyes pop out, but consider the purpose for your printer and the price you're paying before making the final decision.

Thermal Printers

Thermal printers are inexpensive, small, and don't require much voltage to operate. Their drawbacks are that they're slow and can print only on a special waxy paper. (The waxy paper is actually burned by the printer — hence, thermal.) This burned-in image fades with time, usually when the paper is exposed to sunlight. Also, the paper comes primarily on narrow rolls, which doesn't make for impressive correspondence.

Today, thermal printers are a novelty, although some of the laptop computers have them as "portable" options. And thermal printers are good for getting some notes down on hard copy when space, memory, and battery power are important. Still, for the price, better kinds of printers are available.

Laser Printers

Before the introduction of laser printers several years ago, the daisy wheel printer was the final word in office printing. But today, the laser printer provides a *highly* attractive alternative in both price and performance. In fact, all serious computer users should choose a laser printer over any other computer printer any day of the week.

Laser printers are similar to the desktop copying machine, and they work on the same principle. The difference is that the laser printer receives its information from the computer instead of using a reflected image, as does the copy machine. A laser beam is used to draw the image.

Chapter 11: All About Printers

The printed result from a laser printer is impressive. Better than letter quality, laser printers produce what's called "near typeset quality" printing. For example, most typesetting equipment is capable of printing characters at a resolution of 1,200 lines per inch. An affordable laser printer can produce characters at a resolution of 300 lines per inch — one-quarter the resolution at one-sixteenth the cost. Pay a bit more and you can get 400, 600, or even the 1,200 lines per inch that a real typesetting machine can achieve (all in the privacy of your own home or office).

As far as noise is concerned, laser printers are whisper quiet. Odds are the fan in your computer is louder than a laser printer will ever be. Feeding paper into the printer is as easy as putting a sheaf of paper into a tray and sliding it into a slot — just like in a copy machine. Envelopes stick in their own slot. You can even print on your own letterhead simply by substituting the paper. (Sadly, you can't "Xerox your face" with a laser printer.)

Laser printer speed varies. Manufacturers will boast of their printer's speed in terms of *p.p.m.*, pages per minute, with 8 p.p.m. being a good clip, 4 p.p.m. being slow but acceptable, and anything faster than 8 p.p.m. being expensive, er, fastest.

Note that a laser printer's p.p.m. speed, like a dot matrix printer's CPS speed, is not an indication of how fast the printer really works and should be used for comparison purposes only. For example, a speed of 8 p.p.m. is only possible when printing multiple copies of the same page. Because of the amount of calculations the laser printer requires to print a page of text, speeds of 2 or 3 p.p.m. are much more common. Complex documents, with lots of graphics and pictures, could take up to five minutes (or longer) per page to print.

Perhaps the biggest advantage of laser printers over other printer types is their capability to produce graphics. Because the laser printer is basically creating teeny tiny dots on a page, incredible graphics are possible. Depending on the software, graphics and text can be merged on one page. Letters with charts, pictures, different typestyles, and graphs can be done using laser printers. This is all part of that area of computing called desktop publishing (DTP). Complete magazines, brochures, and even computer manuals have been printed using only a computer and a laser printer.

The PC Printer Compatibility Issue

Printers, printers everywhere! So what's the big deal? I felt that way when I went out to buy my second laser printer. The first one cost $4,500. Boy! I wasn't going to make that mistake again! The second one I got on sale for only $1,800. It was a "major brand," so I wasn't worried about finding printer drivers for it.

I was wrong!

Printers (and modems) are one area of computing where brand name labels are worth the premium you pay. The more popular the brand name, the more likely your computer software will recognize your printer and do wondrous things with it.

Presently, there are three printer brands I would consider "standards":

Great Advice ▶ For laser printers and ink jets, Hewlett-Packard printers set the pace. If you buy an "HP" or a printer that's fully compatible with it (meaning that printer will work just like an HP printer without a hitch), then you're in good shape software-wise.

For dot matrix printers, both the IBM and Epson brands carry the most clout.

Almost every software package I've seen supports the Hewlett-Packard, IBM, or Epson printers without any problems. This isn't to say that you should avoid other brand names. Not at all! Instead, just be sure that your software can deal with those printers. If you're certain of that, then compatibility won't be an issue.

✔ Quick Review

As with anything you consider buying for your computer, you have a number of decisions to make when buying a printer. Top priority now is price. If you want a laser printer but would rather spend your money on getting a faster microprocessor, larger hard drive, or more memory, good. Buy a nice, sturdy, and compatible dot matrix printer for now, saving the laser printer purchase for later.

If it's quality you're after, then go with a laser printer. Be sure to find one that *all* of your software recognizes and supports. Refer back to the software worksheets at the front of this book and review your printer notes. Selecting the proper printer based on your software's requirements is vital.

When you've reached your decision, jot down what you want on the hardware worksheet at the front of this book.

One final, important reminder: Printers *do not* come with cables! Remember to buy that one special cable for hooking up your printer to your computer.

CHAPTER 12

Peripherals

Other Items Lurking Around Your Computer That You May Find Necessary

You should have everything you need to make your personal computer complete. Anything extra you might buy is outside of, or *peripheral* to, the main computer box, its keyboard, monitor, and printer. This doesn't mean you don't need any peripherals, or that you won't be interested in buying them later. As you'll soon discover, there are lots of "extras" when it comes to computers.

This chapter touches upon a few of the many things you can add to your computer system. Some of these items you may have heard of before: modems, faxes, networks, multimedia (sound and CD-ROM), and a host of other interesting devices and doodads. So consider this chapter a get-acquainted session for purchases you may make later.

Modems and Faxes

Your computer is all alone in the universe — unless you buy it a *modem* and, through the miracle of the phone company, allow your PC to talk to any other PC also equipped with a modem. This can be done for fun or business, depending on which types of computers you allow your PC to dial up.

> ### The easiest way to install extra goodies in your PC
>
> Suppose that you just have mountains of money and are buying a host of expansion goodies for your PC. Great. I envy you. Now do yourself a favor and buy those things with your computer and make your dealer install and test them for you. This can save you tons of headache later, because installing and adding items to your PC is a major pain.

Modeming opens up an entire world unto itself, full of jargon and mystery. (Indeed, if you think you're cornering the market on computer terminology, then you're in for a surprise when you start to use a modem.) There are three things you should look for in a modem:

- Internal versus external
- Speed (measured in BPS)
- Compatibility

There are other, more technical aspects to a modem as well. In fact, the best advice you can get for buying a modem is to talk with others who use one. They'll probably have some real-life recommendations for you — or some worthy warnings.

Will your modem live inside or outside your PC?

There are two types of modems, internal and external. The internal modem lives inside your PC, plugged into an *expansion slot*. External modems live outside your PC, content in their own daybook-sized box with blinking lights to impress your friends. External modems connect to the computer using a special modem cable, plugging into one of your PC's *serial ports*. Both types of modems connect to the phone jack in your wall with a standard phone cord.

> **GREAT ADVICE**
>
> ### The best modem advice I can offer any human
>
> If you're going to get your PC a modem — and it really can be a lot of fun — then my advice is to have a second phone line, one dedicated to the computer, installed in your home or office.
>
> I'm not pushing this because I own phone company stock. No, it's just *polite*. When others pick up the phone line and the computer is "talking," they get a rude sound in their ears. Further, the act of picking up the phone will disconnect your computer from its conversation. To prevent this, and keep everyone in the house happy, I recommend shelling out the extra $15–30 a month for the computer's own phone line.

The advantage of an internal modem is that it doesn't clutter your desktop. External modems require a power cord and a cable to your PC's serial port; internal modems lack these messy things.

The advantage of an external modem is that you can see its pretty lights and tell exactly what it's up to. You can turn it off by flipping its switch or set its volume using a tiny knob.

Price-wise, internal modems are cheaper because they're just a circuit board you plug into your computer. External modems cost more, and they often lack the "freebie" software that often comes with internal modems.

GREAT ADVICE Personally, I prefer external modems. The reason is that they're portable; you can easily move your modem from one computer to another just by plugging it in. I bought an external modem in 1984 that I've used on a TRS-80, Apple II, Macintosh, IBM PC, and NeXT computer — five different pieces of hardware that could use one modem simply because it was external. An internal modem is pretty much married to the hardware it was designed for. Plus, I like looking at the pretty lights when I go on-line.

Going faster and faster

Modems are measured by their speed, which tells you how fast they can send information through the phone lines. The speed is measured in bits per second or *BPS*. The higher the BPS value, the faster the modem.

In the early days, a 300 BPS modem was about as fast as you could go.

Eventually, prices dropped. Then came the 2400 BPS modem, twice as fast as the 1200 BPS modem, which was the standard for the longest time (and still is about as fast as most modems go). Around 1989, the fast 9600 BPS modems came along, but they were very expensive and fussy. (Some 9600 modems wouldn't talk with other 9600 modems — an issue of compatibility that was eventually ironed out.)

Today, I'd say 9600 BPS modems are the standard, and your best bet is to buy a modem that can go at least that fast. Faster modems will eventually take over the standard. So if you can afford a modem that zooms along at 14K BPS (where the K stands for 1,000) or 28K BPS, go for it. You may have only a few places to call at that speed, but it will certainly swell your chest with pride as you boast of your modem's haste to your on-line friends.

Being Hayes compatible

The final and most important part about getting a modem is to ensure that it's "Hayes compatible." This means that the modem understands the exact same commands used to communicate with the industry-standard Hayes modem. These commands are also referred to as the "AT commands." If your modem claims that compatibility, then you'll never have any problem working with any communications software.

GREAT ADVICE Just as the planet of PC laser printers revolves around the Hewlett-Packard sun, the world of modems orbits the Hayes star. If you pick a Hayes modem, your modem will work with just about any communications software. In fact, Hayes modems traditionally come with the Hayes SmartCom telecommunications software. They're a wee bit more expensive than other modems, but compatibility will never be an issue.

> ### And what of the "Baud rate"?
>
> Sometimes you may hear the term *Baud rate* used instead of, or interchangeably with, BPS. Allow me to clear the air on this one.
>
> A Baud is a scientific term applied to early communication, such as the teletype. The first modems in the late '70s used the term to apply to information sent by computers. However, as computer communication evolved on its own, the term BPS (bits per second) became a more accurate and useful description of how information was being sent. So between the two, BPS is correct. Baud is often used interchangeably, though it's technically incorrect. You have my permission to slap anyone who refers to a "Baud rate" when talking about a modem.

If you can't afford Hayes, or just don't like them, feel free to select any other modem. Always insist upon Hayes compatibility and double-check your communications software to ensure that it understands and appreciates the modem you've selected.

The whole fax/modem deal

A fax/modem is nothing more than a traditional modem that can also be used to send and receive faxes, just like a fax machine. Obviously, having fax features in your modem will add to its price. Is it worth it? It depends.

The advantage of a fax/modem is that you can use your word processor (or whatever software) to send a fax without ever having to print anything. For example, if I wanted to send an irate letter to my publisher, I would have to write it out in my word processor, print it, then gently feed it into my fax machine. With a fax/modem attached to my PC, I just choose the command to send a fax in my word processor, and what I've written is faxed automatically — without ever using paper. (Of course, it's a little more complex than that, but that's generally how it works.)

Receiving faxes is a little different. Unlike a real fax machine that prints the fax out on paper, a fax/modem saves the fax's image on your computer's hard drive. You can use special software to view the fax or print it after it's received. Personally, I prefer to get my faxes on paper using a real fax machine, but if you have a fax/modem, you don't have to bother with that step.

GREAT ADVICE As with all computer hardware, to make a fax/modem work you need software. Before buying a certain fax/modem, check out PC fax software. See which other types of software it works with (to ensure that all your software can send faxes). Then check the list of fax/modems that the software likes. Use that list to help you narrow down your fax/modem purchase.

Multimedia and Sound

Multimedia is the current buzz word for adding a sound card and CD-ROM drive to your computer. With those two devices, your computer can play music, talk to you, and play videos or animation, and you'll have hours of fun toying with interesting new computer games, virtual reality, the whole nine yards.

There are really only two key elements needed to make a multimedia system:

- A sound card
- A CD-ROM drive

Though your PC has a speaker, it can only beep and bleat through it. To get better sound, you need a *sound card* for your PC. This is an expansion card that allows your computer to become a synthesizer and play its own music, to play recorded music and recorded voices, or to synthesize its own voice. External speakers can be used to hear the sound, or you can use headphones to be quiet; or just plug the darn thing into your stereo system if you want to alarm the neighbors.

The second part of a multimedia PC consists of a CD-ROM drive. The CD stands for Compact Disc, and they're exactly the same as the CDs you buy in a record store, except computer CDs have programs and other data on them, not necessarily just music.

Almost all CD-ROM drives require a SCSI controller to operate. This is the same SCSI controller used to control a hard drive plus a host of other peripherals. So if you've decided on a SCSI controller for your hard drive, all you need to do is buy a compatible CD-ROM drive and you're in business. Otherwise, CD-ROM drives may come with optional SCSI controllers. And some sound cards may even include custom SCSI controllers for a CD-ROM drive.

GREAT ADVICE The easy solution to all this multimedia madness is to buy a multimedia upgrade kit. This is what I recommend, and it's often cheaper than buying all the pieces separately. The upgrade kit comes with a sound card, CD-ROM drive, all the cables and connectors, plus some "free" multimedia software.

Multimedia upgrade kits can typically be purchased when you buy your computer (and have your dealer install it for you), or you can opt to buy a specific multimedia computer. These are basically standard PCs, though they have the multimedia upgrade kit included in the price.

And what is that price? Expect to pay anywhere from $400 to $900 extra for multimedia, depending on how sophisticated you want your upgrade kit. Here, I would recommend avoiding some of the top-of-the-line stuff unless your goal is to produce multimedia software.

The sound card compatibility issue

There are lots of PC sound cards on the market, but two names crop up more than any of the others: SoundBlaster and AdLib.

If you go with either the SoundBlaster or AdLib brand names, great. Otherwise, ensure that your sound card is *very* compatible with one or the other.

Really boring CD-ROM technical tidbits

The only technical tidbit you really need to know about buying a CD-ROM drive is that the faster ones are better. They're graded in speeds, such as 2X or 3X (which may also be called double-spin or triple-spin) or whatever. Always try to buy the fastest CD-ROM you can afford.

Also, try to buy a CD-ROM drive that uses a SCSI controller. You may be lucky and already have a SCSI controller in your computer, or you may have one included with your multimedia sound card. Try to avoid CD-ROMs with their own *proprietary* controller.

Two other items worth noting are *access time* and *data transfer rate*. As with a hard drive, access time measures the speed of the drive. For a CD-ROM, avoid anything slower (that is, greater than) 200 ms. Also, look for a CD-ROM drive that has a data transfer rate of 300K per second or higher. Anything slower (that is, less than 300K) is terribly annoying.

> ### What's that? Can't hear you?
>
> Sound cards are great, but you need speakers or a set of headphones to hear what they're squawking. And, needless to say, sound cards typically don't come with either. Be sure to ask before you assemble your multimedia system. Expect to pay from $5 up to $*a lot* for headphones or a decent speaker system. And don't skimp here! Nice speakers can really make your PC sound system.

Other Peripherals: Optical Disks, Tape Backup Units, Scanners, and Backup Power Supplies

The list of things you can buy for your computer is endless. You'll discover this for yourself as your credit card bill gets larger and larger in the coming months.

The following is just a brief list of things you can buy for your computer. My advice here is to wait until you have your basic system assembled before you consider any of these; try not to overwhelm yourself with too much hardware, or your mind will truly get boggled.

> ### And now, the sad news: Multimedia means 486 or greater
>
> In order to do multimedia right on a PC, you'll need a fast computer. I recommend buying at least a 486 microprocessor that hums along at a minimum of 33 MHz. Anything slower and your multimedia software will suffer.
>
> Also, you need very good video to do multimedia right. Insist on the best quality SVGA or XGA graphics you can afford with at least 1MB (preferably 2MB) of video memory.

Strange and wonderful disk drives

The first urge of early hard drive users was to vigorously yank their "fixed disks" from their computers. After all, before hard drives, there were only floppy drives, and you could easily remove their disks from the computer to store them or just keep them with you. I suppose no one trusted the first hard drives. So one of the first wacky disk drives to come out was a removable hard drive.

Removable hard drives still have their lure. They allow you to use several different disks in one drive, which means you get more storage. In other words, one hard drive with six 250MB removable disks means you have 1,500MB of total storage. What a deal! You can also move the disks from one computer to another, so you'll always have "your stuff" with you.

Another type of wonderful disk is the WORM or MO drive. The *O* stands for *optical,* and these drives actually store information optically instead of magnetically — like a CD versus a recorded cassette tape.

WORM is not only a cool acronym, it really stands for something: Write Once, Read Many. It's an optical disk that you can write to once but can read any number of times. This disk is ideal for archiving or storing information long-term that you don't want accidentally erased.

MO stands for Magneto-Optical. This is a type of optical drive that works like more traditional disk drives, where you can write many times and read many times. These drives are expensive, but the information stored on them is almost indestructible.

Tape backup systems

Backup is the art of making safety copies of your stuff. This sounds wonderful. Imagine making a backup of all your possessions in case of theft or fire. If anything happens to the originals, the backups are identical copies. You would think computer people would be nuts about making backups. Wrong!

A tape backup system works a lot like a cassette tape (and it sort of looks like one, too). You stick the tape into a special tape drive and then run special software to back up your hard drive. A few minutes later, all your stuff is copied to the tape as a safety, backup copy.

> **GREAT ADVICE** I recommend that everyone get a tape backup drive, though it's not a necessary part of your initial computer purchase. As with all hardware, first look for backup software and discover what types of tape drives the software works best with. Then go out and buy your tape backup drive. Also, remember to buy the tape cassettes of the proper size and shape for your drive.

Scanning for gold

A nifty device to add to any computer is a scanner. This is a Xerox machine-like thing that reads an image — photograph, page from a book, document, your face, whatever — and translates it into a graphic image that you see on the computer screen. With the proper kind of software, you can even edit the image and do all sorts of wondrous and wacky things with it.

> **GREAT ADVICE** Try to get a scanner you can plug into a SCSI port on your PC. Some scanners have proprietary expansion cards required to make them work. Avoid them. Also try to get a "single pass" type of scanner that will be much more efficient than the multi-pass models.

Protecting your investment with a special power supply

Finally, a real good friend you should consider buying as a PC companion is a *power protector* or *UPS*, uninterruptible power supply.

Power protectors come in all shapes and sizes. But first, don't confuse a power protector with a *power strip*. A power strip, sometimes called a *power bar*, is simply a gang of outlets hanging on the end of an extension cord. It offers very little protection for your computer from the evils of surges, spikes, line noise, and other nasty electrical things that can damage your PC's delicate innards.

A power protector usually has a noise filter or spike protector. The idea is that if anything nasty comes out of your wall socket, the power protector will "eat it" first, before it can damage your PC.

A UPS is actually a battery you plug your PC into. In the event of a blackout, your computer continues to run smoothly from the battery. Of course, it can only run for a few minutes, so the idea is to save your stuff, shut down the computer, and then wait for the power to come back on again.

GREAT ADVICE ▸ Speaking from personal experience, you should definitely invest in a UPS for your computer. I lost a $1,000 hard drive in 1990 because the power flickered for about three seconds. Anywhere the power is even slightly unreliable, you should connect your computer and its monitor to a UPS. I can't recommend it more.

✔ Quick Review

Peripherals are fun. You can add them to your computer to personalize your system as well as extend its abilities.

If you've spotted any peripheral you like, make a note of it on the worksheet at the front of this book. I've listed these items last since they are, after all, extras. If money is tight, seriously consider buying your peripherals at a later date (though it doesn't hurt to prepare for them now, for example, by getting a SCSI interface).

Also, be aware that many peripherals require software to work properly. So if you're planning on getting a modem or tape backup for your PC, look at communications and backup software to see what you like. Then find the compatible peripheral.

Chapter 13

Shopping for Service and Support

Never Underestimate This Important Step!

You should take five steps to buy a computer. So far you've done three: You've decided what you want your computer to do; you've found the software that will get that job done; and you've just completed a survey of computer hardware, matching it up to your software needs. The next step is to prepare for shopping. By that, I mean *prepare*. Don't go shopping yet!

Before you even think about looking at a computer ad, you need to find some place that will give you the proper service and support. Even before you go shopping, you should think about what happens *after* the sale. In some cases, I consider this more important than making a deal. In fact, it's the fourth step in buying a computer: Look for service and support. The people who are the most disappointed with buying a computer are the ones who omit this important step.

Finding Service and Support for Your PC

The biggest mistake people make when they buy a computer is shopping for price and not service or support. Lack of those two important items can be a real cost. A dealer makes his reputation on service and not on the lowest price. (This is why two dealers will sell the same equipment at different prices.)

Often, the lowest-priced computer advertised is not a good first-time buy. Although low price does not imply a *rip off*, it *can* imply little or no service.

Most computer dealers do not stock junk. They are always sure to carry those items that give them the least amount of headaches. Dealers don't want to see you coming back with problems all the time; they want happy customers.

Service means *where does it get fixed*

The first thing you should ask a dealer is, "Where do I get my computer fixed?" The best answer is, "Right here!" The worst answer is, "At our automated overseas factory!"

When you buy a new computer, you want to make sure that you know where to take it if it breaks. Or, better yet, find out if the store exchanges the broken computer for a new one. Some places do this but only for a limited time after the sale. Otherwise, make sure the dealer has his own fix-it place.

Check the warranty

Never buy any computer equipment unless it has a warranty. In fact, you may find that most stuff comes with two warranties: one from the manufacturer and another from the person who sells you the product. So you may find a monitor with a 90-day warranty from the manufacturer and your dealer may bring that up to a year, all at no charge.

> ### Keep in mind that computers take time to fix
>
> Unless you have an on-site service contract (which should come *free* when you buy your computer), you're going to have to take it into the shop to get fixed. O! What an experience, let me tell you....
>
> Expect these places to take a while to fix your computer. I've known of PCs in the shop for five days or more. The rule of thumb is, "The busier the store, the longer it will take to get your PC fixed."
>
> If you're fortunate, some dealers may offer *loaners* while your PC is in the shop. This may be part of an extended service contract (which I don't recommend you get; though if having a loaner is important to you, you should consider it).

The reason for a warranty is to *work the bugs out*. Electronic components — if they break at all — will usually break right away, typically well under 30 days after purchase. For most stuff, that's well within the warranty period.

Service contracts are nice — unless you pay for them

Here's a healthy warning: Do not bother with maintenance agreements. Inquire only if knowing helps you sleep better at night. For most computers, the warranty period is fair. No matter what dealers say, don't waste your money on an extended maintenance program. You'll probably wind up paying from $100 to $250 for it and you won't ever need it.

The two most common things that break in a computer are the disk drive and power supply. If either of these breaks during the warranty period (usually one month to a year, depending on where you buy your machine), you get it replaced for free. If either breaks after the warranty period, the cost for each is usually far less than any maintenance agreement. So think hard before purchasing one. You'll just be putting more money into someone else's pocket.

The *burn-in* process

Some dealers will actually pretest your equipment for you. This is known as a *burn-in test,* because they assemble the computer and then run it through a battery of tests for typically a 24-hour period. They do this so they can find any bugs or quirks first, before you find them. Then the stuff is automatically repaired or replaced before you ever see the machine.

If a dealer offers a burn-in for new equipment, consider it a bonus. (And don't complain because of the extra delivery time.) If they don't offer it, ask. And if they still say no, don't think of it as any big deal. Chapter 15 will tell you how to do your own burn-in to safely find anything wrong well into the first warranty period.

How long is a *lifetime warranty*?

I love the phrase *lifetime warranty*. Whose lifetime is it? Do they mean the product's lifetime? In that case, if the product *dies,* does the warranty go with it? Or do they mean your lifetime?

The absolute bottom line on lifetime warranties is the company that sold you the product. If it goes belly-up, the warranty dies, too. Obviously this should encourage you to buy from a reputable dealer. Friendly Joe selling from the back of his pickup truck at the swap meet may claim to be there every weekend, but . . . you get the idea.

For reputable dealers, a lifetime warranty is more an expression of trust than a warranty. Like most electronics, things will break right away, usually within 30 or 90 days. Anything that busts after that will probably die of old age, which you may find as the ultimate definition of *lifetime warranty.*

Support means *help me* after the sale

Besides inquiring about service from a computer dealer, ask about support. What kind of support does the dealer offer? Who can you call with a question? Often, you may find the dealer to be very friendly. However, after you sign your check, some dealers *may* pretend they've never heard of you.

Where can you go when you have trouble? A great bonus is to have hands-on training included in the purchase price. In some cases, the dealer has a small classroom where you can sit down with your computer and learn all about it. A hands-on class is best because you can learn more by making your own mistakes (and you will!).

The question usually asked at this point is, "Where can I learn all this stuff — about service and support?"

The answer is to shop around and ask a lot of questions. Although it would be unfair of me to recommend one dealer over another, I can direct you to local *User Groups*. Find users who are interested in the computer you plan on buying, ask them questions, and listen to what they've heard. Sure, there are a lot of war stories out there, but some people might nudge you toward the dealer that's just right for you. (Refer to Appendix B for more information on User Groups.)

The Dealer Service and Support Worksheet

To help you with your task of finding service and support, I've concocted a Service and Support Survey worksheet, shown in Figure 13-1. Take this worksheet (or a copy) along with you as you visit or phone various dealers, shopping for service and support. You can then use this sheet later to help you choose the dealer who offers your desired level of service and support.

Dealer name. Write down the dealer's name here.

Where repaired. Where is your computer repaired. Give three points if it is fixed right there in the shop; give two if it's at another location cross-town. If it is shipped away to be fixed, give one point. Zero points are awarded if it's shipped away and you pay the shipping.

Warranty. Give the dealers one point for every 90 days in their own warranty. So if they give a year warranty — above and beyond the product's warranty (and it must be above and beyond) — give them four points. A two-year bonus warranty would be eight points. No extra warranty gets a zero.

Burn-in. Do dealers burn-in or test the equipment. Most places don't because they see it as unnecessary. Give the dealers one point for a burn-in test, otherwise give them zero.

Service contract. This item counts only if you plan on getting a service contract. If the service contract is around $120 per year, give two points. Any more expensive, give fewer points; any less expensive, give three points. (This is an item you'll need to use your own best judgment on since I don't recommend service contracts in the first place.)

Dealer Name	Where Repaired	Warranty	Burn-In	Service Contract	On-Site Service	Level of Support	Class-room	Phone Calls	Total

Service and Support Survey

Figure 13-1: Service and Support Survey.

On-site service. If the dealers offer on-site service for free, give them two points. If on-site service is extra and determined, for example, on a per-visit basis, give them one point. If they don't offer on-site service, it's zero.

Level of support. How amiable are they to helping you out? Rate them from one to ten, with ten being best. Give more points if they are willing to answer phone calls, talk with you in person, offer classes, or just appear friendly. This is a chance to express your own feelings.

Classroom. Do the dealers have a classroom? If so, give them three points. If they're in cahoots with a local college or business, give them two points. If they charge for the classes, give them one point. No classes earns a zero.

Phone calls. This is primarily for mail-order computers. If it's 800 (toll-free) numbers for everything, then give them a three. If you can use 800 numbers but only for a limited time, then they get a two. Toll calls get a one when the support is free. If you must pay for the call as well as the support, give them a zero.

Total. Add up your dealer's score. Anything between 10 and 25 is considered acceptable, with higher numbers always better. Avoid any place with a score of 10 or less.

You may find that a lot of dealers don't offer the perks, such as classrooms and on-site support, primarily to save you money. However, consider the importance of those items and your own personal level of service and support when you make your final decision to buy.

✔ Quick Review

The best way you can guarantee a lousy first-time computer-buying experience is to neglect service and support. Forget cheap prices. What you need is someone to help you when you get stuck; someone who won't run for cover when you come back with a question . . . for the sixth time!

Service means *where does it get fixed?* Hopefully, it's right there and right away, though busy stores have long turnaround times. Service also means a good warranty, plus the benefits of a burn-in and on-site service if offered. Avoid service contracts unless the thought of living without one makes you numb.

Support means your dealer will be there to help you after the sale. Your dealer should accept phone calls and in-person visits, offer help and classes, and do it all without balking.

Find the proper service and support, and you're only one step away from buying your new computer.

Chapter 14
Buying Your Computer

Go for It!

Buying a computer. Find someone whose fingernails have been chewed to the nubs and they've probably been looking for a computer. Simply mention *buying a computer* to anyone, especially someone who is currently looking, and they'll probably faint — maybe even die.

Fortunately, you've read this book and are more than ready to buy a computer. In fact, waiting for this chapter was probably the only thing keeping you in your chair.

Putting It All Together

Shown at the very beginning of this book is the worksheet you've been filling in, detailing the requirements of your hardware purchase. You've selected the components of your computer based on your software's appetite. This worksheet should list the minimum hardware requirements of the computer to meet your needs.

This worksheet you've filled out will look similar to something your dealer may have. A sample of one such worksheet is shown in Figure 14-1. As the salesperson in this store figures out what you need, he will fill in various parts of the worksheet so that the shop *in the back* can assemble your computer.

59053

Datel
Systems Incorporated
Todays Computers Business Center

☐ 4444 Convoy St.., Ste. 300, San Diego, CA 92111
(619) 571-3100 • FAX: 571-0452
☐ 740 Nordahl Rd., Ste. 122, San Marcos, CA 92069
(619) 740-0344 • FAX: 740-0805
☐ 8624 Cuyamaca St., Santee, CA 92071
(619) 562-1420 • FAX: 562-1331
☐ Service: (619) 571-7411 • FAX: 569-9970

☐ **Quote** Date: / / ☐ **Order** Date: / / ☐ **Required** Date: / /

Salesperson: Terms: ☐ Taxable P.O.# Buyer:

Sold to:	**Ship to:**
Name	Name
Attention	Attention
Address	Address
City State Zip	City State Zip
Phone Day Eve	Phone Day Eve
FAX	FAX

☐ Datel 286	Drive 1:	☐ 360K	☐ 1.2MB	☐ 720K	☐ 1.44MB	☐ 2.88MB
☐ Datel 386 SX	Drive 2:	☐ 360K	☐ 1.2MB	☐ 720K	☐ 1.44MB	☐ 2.88MB
☐ Datel 386 DX	Hard Drive:	☐ Capacity		Brand		
☐ Datel 486 DX	RAM:	☐ 1MB	☐ 2MB	☐ 4MB	☐ 8MB	☐ Other
☐ IBM PS2	Video:	☐ Mono	☐ VGA	☐ SVGA	Brand	RAM
☐ Other	Ports:	☐ Serial	☐ Parallel	☐ Game	☐ Clock	☐ Math
	☐ Monitor			☐ Tape		
☐ Case	☐ Network			☐ Modem		
☐ DOS	☐ Mouse		☐ Keyboard		☐ Other	

Qty	Description	Price	Total

Comments: **Subtotal**

Tax

Page__ of __ **Shipping**

When Ready: ☐ Pickup ☐ UPS ☐ Truck **TOTAL**

Original - Construction Yellow - Purchasing Pink - Sales Goldenrod - Buyer

Figure 14-1: A worksheet for buying a computer.

Now that you know what you want and you've looked for service and support, you're ready to start shopping. That's done by looking at prices and seeing what's out there.

Buying more than what you need

Buying anything above and beyond what you have written down depends on how much you can afford. So the real question you ask is, "Where should I spend my money first?"

Without a doubt, spend any extra money you may have on the following items in order:

1. Microprocessor
2. Hard drive
3. Memory

First and foremost, buy yourself a faster microprocessor if you can afford it. This is a must. If your software only craves a 386, buy a 486 or Pentium if you can afford it.

Second, buy a higher capacity hard drive. If you've followed the hard drive size-equation from Chapter 8 and can afford a large hard drive, buy it.

The last item you can splurge on is memory. I list this last because, of the three, it's the easiest to add later (to *upgrade*).

When will I get my PC?

It's very rare that you go to buy a computer and walk out of the store with one that day. If you'll review Figure 14-1, note the item, *Required Date*. This is because it takes time to assemble your own personal computer. If you're lucky, the store may have one sitting right there in the back, ready to be loaded into your car. But most of the time, plan on waiting anywhere from a couple of hours to several days for your computer, depending on how busy the place is and whether or not they run tests on your computer before giving it to you. (More on that in the next chapter.)

> **Don't ever put a deposit down on a computer!**
>
> Warning! When dealers ask you for a deposit up front, run like the wind! Up-front deposits are one surefire way to find a shady computer dealer. You should never put down a deposit on a computer. Sure, some places may ring up your bill before delivery or a couple of days before the computer is assembled. If so, refuse to pay until delivery or pay with a credit card. You can always cancel orders on your credit card if it turns out to be a rip-off. But don't pay cash or by check. Some unethical dealers use a *rob-Peter-to-pay-Paul* scheme to finance their operations. It happens all the time! Above all, don't pay in advance if the wait is more than one or two days for the machine — especially if the dealer's reputation is in doubt.
>
> Incidentally, don't fret over having to put a deposit down to hold a special on-order item. For example, you may need some special piece of equipment not in stock. If so, a 5 to 20 percent deposit is okay to hold it for you. Again, use the dealer's reputation as the deciding factor.

Reading a Computer Ad

The first step in buying that computer is to look at computer ads. This can be boring, but it's definitely not as boring as browsing in a warehouse-sized computer store. After all, you're going to show up knowing exactly what you need; you don't need to be sold anything. Computer stores aren't really set up for that kind of customer (just look around next time you visit a store).

Figure 14-2 shows a typical computer ad, something that I mocked up myself this morning. It shows various systems along with their hardware contents and prices.

First, realize that the systems displayed are primarily set up for price comparison with competitors. You can assemble any PC you want with any microprocessor, any amount of memory, any size hard drive — whatever your needs are. So don't be put off by a place because it may not have your personal computer right there in the ad.

CHAPTER 14: BUYING YOUR COMPUTER

```
===============================================================
                    Jerry's PC Hut
===============================================================
   Super Bargains!              Super Deals!
```

Super 486SX PC Deal   **Super Dooper 486/66DX**   **Super Dooper Pentium!**

- 486SX, 25mhz
- 8MB RAM
- 340MB Hard drive
- SuperVGA Graphics
- Super VGA Monitor
- 3½-inch, 1.4M disk drive
- Klakity 101 Keyboard
- MS Mouse
- MS-DOS 6.22 & Windows

$1195

- 486DX, 66mhz
- 8MB RAM
- 520MB H.D.D. (12 ms)
- PCI Video w/1MB VRAM
- Super VGA Monitor
- 3½-inch, 1.4M disk drive
- Klakity 101 Keyboard
- MS Mouse
- MS-DOS 6.22 & Windows

$1395

- Pentium, 90mhz
- 8MB RAM
- 528MB H.D.D. (12 ms)
- PCI Video w/2MB VRAM
- Super 17" Monitor
- 3½-inch, 1.4M disk drive
- Klakity 101 Keyboard
- MS Mouse
- MS-DOS 6.22 & Windows

$1895

Other Super Options:
Multimedia upgrade kit $459.00
    Includes Sound Blaster-compatible
    sound card, Speakers 2X CD-ROM,
    Software, CDs and drivers!
RAM Upgrade .... $CALL!
Super 21" Sony Monitor $1395.00
Super SCSI/2 1G drive! $1200.00
Temecula Tape Backup $240.00

Jerry's PC Hut
M-F 10:00 - 8:30
Sat 9:00 - 6:00
Closed Sunday!
(We go to Church!)
909-555-1899
909-555-1940 FAX
Call our BBS!
909-555-0123, 9600BPS, 8-N-1

Call for the latest prices on our vast selection of printers, scanners, modems, other stuff and PC and Windows Software! We have shareware! More than anyone else. Promise.

You'd be a dope to shop anywhere else!

Figure 14-2: A typical computer ad.

Second, notice that the ads use a lot of abbreviations. I'm sure that some fondness for computer jargon is responsible, but most likely it's space restrictions that cause *RAM* to be used instead of *memory, MB* or *M* for *megabytes,* and even *H.D.D.* for *a hard disk drive. VRAM* is *Video RAM* or *Video Memory.* And often you'll find customized products, such as the *Klakity* keyboard or maybe some special type of mouse.

Third, some items are missing from the computer's descriptions. For example, should you assume that the computer has a serial and printer port? I would ask.

Finally, don't forget the service and support! It may not say anything about what's offered in the ad, so be sure to phone or visit the store before you make a decision.

133

Where to Buy

Looking over a few ads will give you an idea of what's out there. But eventually you'll have to pick a few places to phone or visit and get a more lasting impression. Remember, you don't want to shop by price alone. A store's reputation is based on service and support, which you can't tell over the phone.

When it comes time to narrow down your choices, you'll find that there are four types of places where you can buy your computer:

- A local computer store
- A national chain store
- A megastore
- Mail order

Any of these are fine by me for buying a first-time computer. Even mail-order places offer service and support, though the support is over the phone instead of in a classroom.

> ### Common tricks used to make the advertised price look really cheap
>
> Competition is fierce out there, so computer dealers will go to great lengths to make their systems look cheaper than the other guys. Here are some common tricks you may want to look for or inquire about when you find a ridiculous price:
>
> - Not adding any memory to the computer. Look for 0K RAM or 0M RAM in the ads, or maybe the memory value is missing altogether.
> - Not adding in the price of the keyboard.
> - Not adding in the price of the monitor or video adapter card.
> - Not adding in the microprocessor (this sounds ridiculous, but it happens).
> - Not adding in the operating system. Technically, this should be *thrown in,* but the dealer may be saving a few bucks by not including it.
> - *Omitting support or service!*

CHAPTER 14: BUYING YOUR COMPUTER

> ### Getting a quote
>
> Most stores will offer a *meet or beat* way to price a computer. They'll claim to meet or beat any advertised price on the same or similar equipment. If this is the way you like to shop, then get several quotes from different sources before you buy. (You'll notice the quote box in the worksheet in Figure 14-1).
>
> Don't forget to factor in a few dollars for service and support when comparing prices. There is always some hole-in-the-wall place that will want your business when you buy. But will it want to see you again when you have a question or need help?

Your locally owned and operated computer store

If you're one to support the local economy, then a locally owned store will probably be your first choice. These places may look tacky. They may have stuff on Price Club tables and boxes stacked in the back. But they may also have fair prices and an owner who offers more personal support than his Big Brother competitors.

> ### Can I haggle?
>
> The days of haggling when buying a computer are long gone. It used to be that computers were marked up so much that only a complete nebbish would pay list price. You could typically count on a 20 to 50 percent mark-up in the swankier stores.
>
> Today, the competition between stores is too great to allow for any haggling. The price you see advertised is usually what the computer sells for. There is still a manufacturer's suggested retail price (MSRP). You may find that ridiculous value written above the store's *discount price*. Whatever. Don't expect to get any more breaks than that.

135

> **Don't forget your software!**
>
> Your computer needs an operating system! Your computer needs software! Software is, after all, the reason why you're buying a computer in the first place.
>
> Refer to the chart at the front of this book for a list of the software you must purchase along with your PC hardware. *You need both!*

The most serious issue you should concern yourself with regarding a local store is how long it has been in business. Any store that's been around for three years or more probably has an excellent reputation (or at least a reputation that you can verify). New places should be given a chance as well, but consider hanging out in the lobby or checking the service counter to see if there are any disgruntled customers. You might also ask for a list of satisfied customers to confirm its reputation.

National chains

The national computer stores aren't what they used to be. Those upscale, haughty computer stores of the late '80s suffered when the smart shopper realized those stores carried the same stuff as the local and discount stores, plus they charged a premium and offered very little in return.

Today when you talk about national chains, you usually mean places like Sears, Radio Shack, KMART, Costco, Sam's, and other places that carry a bunch of stuff other than computers.

The big benefit of buying a computer at a national chain is that they're everywhere. Unlike local dealers, you'll never have to worry about finding a Radio Shack or Sears since they're all over.

The big drawback to these places is that they're not geared specifically toward helping people buy computers. Some places are exceptions, but mostly you'll find computers stacked next to Nintendo game machines and C&W compact discs. There won't be a classroom to teach you DOS or Windows, and don't expect to get far when you phone them up to ask a question about formatting a disk.

The megastore

Megastores are those super computer stores, some bigger than your grocery store, that have everything and anything to do with a computer. There you can browse, check out new hardware, ask questions, take classes, and spend money until you have to take out a third mortgage.

Megastores are quickly replacing the mom-and-pop local dealers and national chains as *the* place to go for computers. They offer substantial discounts, usually have on-site service and support, and everything is in stock.

One downfall I've found with these stores is that the staff turns over too quickly. Just as I make a reputation with someone, they're off someplace else. This is a minor quibble as long as the new clerk is just as knowledgeable as the guy he's replacing.

Be sure to check on warranties, return policies, and double-check on the service and support before you commit to one of these stores.

Mail-order brand names

Welcome to the 1990s where you can have just about anything mailed to your house — including a computer! You typically order from a catalog or magazine article, the company quotes you, and a few days or weeks later your computer shows up ready to go.

Mail-order computers offer the same things as your local dealer or megastore. The only difference is that the computer is sent to your home or office instead of to a loading dock. Often the price is cheaper because there is no in-store markup and often you can dodge your state's sales tax (though I'm not actually coming out and recommending that).

Many people are concerned about mail-order computers showing up dead or damaged. Before you order, make sure that there is a *no-questions-asked* return policy and that the manufacturer pays (or reimburses you) for shipping. You'll find that most places have such polices and, even so, rarely does equipment arrived damaged.

About the only downside to mail-order computers is that your support is over the phone. Most places offer you an 800 number that you can call just about anytime to ask a question. However, if you're more comfortable with in-person support, consider a local dealer or megastore.

One other perk to look for is free on-site service. This is especially important if you live or work in the boonies, as I do. Make sure that the mail-order company offers this service even after the warranty period is up, and double-check that your city and state are included in the deal.

Mail-order pieces parts

There is a difference between a mail-order brand name computer and what I call a mail-order pieces parts computer. That is, no one should buy a mail-order pieces parts computer as their first computer. Instead, if you're going to go mail order, buy a brand name you know: Apple, Compaq, Dell, Gateway, IBM, Micron, Zeos, and a host of others that I don't have time to list.

The main way you can tell a pieces parts mail-order outfit is that it sells pieces parts in addition to complete computer systems. So right along with its main Pentium and 486 systems, you'll see a list of hard drives, memory, video cards, modems, printers, and other stock ready to roll. Sure, those prices look good, but if it doesn't offer the kind of service and support you need, why bother?

And the Final Step Is To . . .

Go for it! When you're finally ready to buy, take a deep breath and follow these steps:

Review the results you want from the computer. How is it going to be used — for business? education? entertainment? work? A computer is a major purchase, not to be taken lightly.

Next, find the software that will best get the job done. The software controls the hardware! Nothing is more depressing than finding people who buy a discount PC because it is cheap only to discover that they need a larger hard drive, more memory, and a new microprocessor to run their favorite software. Shop for the software you need and *then* find the matching computer.

Chapter 14: Buying Your Computer

After you've found the computer to run your software, locate a reputable dealer who offers the service and support you need. Some people don't need support. New computer users must have it. Keep in mind that the dealer's reputation is made on the service it offers.

Now you have your software, know which computer you want, and have found the degree of service and support ideal for you. The final step is to do it! Buy that computer!

Twelve common mistakes made by first-time computer buyers

1. Not knowing what you want the computer to do.
2. Buying hardware instead of software.
3. Shopping for the cheapest computer system in town.
4. Being unprepared for the sale.
5. Not buying extra floppy disks.
6. Not reading the set-up manuals.
7. Forgetting that software is expensive.
8. Not looking for a printer.
9. Forgetting to buy a printer cable.
10. Not buying printer paper.
11. Buying too much.
12. Not counting learning time.

✔ Quick Review

Gather your software worksheets from the front of this book and buy what you need. Use the Service and Support Survey from Chapter 13 to find a dealer. Then use the hardware worksheet from the front of this book to buy your computer. Do it!

Chapter 15

About Your Computer System

Learning to Love It or Hate It

The five steps may be over, and you probably have a new computer sitting in front of you. Congratulations — you won't be disappointed. But first you need to make sure that everything works. This is where you start to put some of the service and support from your dealer to the test. Hopefully, nothing will go wrong, and most of the time that's the case.

If you haven't yet put your computer together, then this chapter will offer you some helpful hints and strategies. If your computer is fully assembled and up and running, skim ahead to the section titled "Breaking It In (the 'Burn-In' Test)" for some helpful hints on putting your computer's wee li'l rubber feet to the fire.

Setting Up Your PC

Unless the nice person you bought it from set up your computer right there on your desk, you'll have to do it yourself. This is much easier than it was in the early days. The first Apple computer (which cost $666 in 1977, by the way) came as a bag of diodes and electronic parts. You soldered the whole thing together from scratch! Today, assembling a PC is more of a plug-and-go operation. You may not even need a screwdriver since most everything has thumb-tighteners now.

Computers come in boxes. There will probably be two big ones: one for the computer's monitor and another for the computer box itself. You may have other boxes as well, depending on your computer's manufacturer and how many peripherals you bought.

If there's a box that screams "Open me first!" then open it first. It probably contains instructions. Otherwise, open the biggest box first and look for the instructions.

Finding all the pieces parts

After you find the instructions, locate the sheet that lists all the parts that came with your computer. This may also be on your invoice or packing list. Try to find all the parts to make sure that you've got 'em. Nothing is more distressing than discovering you're missing a part on Saturday and having to wait until late Monday to use your PC.

Also, don't panic if you can't find some small computer part (like the keyboard) when unpacking your computer. These beasts come in lots of boxes, and boxes within boxes. Look everywhere before calling your dealer and accusing him of omitting something.

Putting the darn thing together

Each computer is different, but there are some standard ways that things are put together.

First, just about everything has a plug that plugs into the wall. Your monitor, computer box, printer, and anything else peripheral (such as a modem) need to plug into a wall socket. Because of this, I recommend buying one of those *power strips* that allow you to plug four, six, or more items into one receptacle. An even better deal is to get a *power protector* or *UPS* (see Chapter 12 for more information).

> ### Save your boxes!
>
> It's a good idea to save the box your computer came in, along with any packing material or "stuffing." This is so you can easily ship the computer back to the store or the mail order company in case it's defective.
>
> How long should you hang on to the box? It's okay to toss it out after the warranty period, typically 30 to 90 days. If you move a lot, then moving companies love it when you have your computer boxes for shipping. And if you're a pack rat, just keep 'em forever.

Chapter 15: About Your Computer System

> ### "Do I have to read the manuals?"
>
> Nope. But I recommend looking over all the manuals just to see what you've got. There may be a humorous tutorial or guide for assembling your PC. Also, keep all the manuals together — in one spot — so you can read them later... if you dare!

Before plugging anything else in, make sure that everything is turned off! You don't want to plug something into the computer when everything is turned on. This may damage the electronic components. So double-check to make sure that you have everything switched off at this point. (For switches with symbols that look like l and O, the l means "on.")

Second, the monitor plugs into the back of the computer box. There will be a *port* labeled "monitor" or "VGA" or "display" or something similar. Plug your monitor's cable into that.

Third, the keyboard plugs into the computer box somewhere. Because the keyboard sits in front of the computer box, you would assume the connection is on the front. Don't expect it to be that logical, though. Most keyboard connectors are on your computer's rump (which doesn't mean that's where the keyboard goes).

Fourth, if you bought a mouse, plug it into the proper port on the back of your computer box. The mouse sits in front of your computer next to the keyboard with its cable, or tail, pointing away from you. Southpaws like the mouse on the left; otherwise put it on the right.

Fifth, if you bought a printer, plug its printer cable into its back. Then plug the other end of the cable into the back of your computer box. You'll notice that the cable has different funny ends, only one of which will plug into the printer or computer box.

Finally, anything else that you bought also needs to be plugged into the computer box. For example, an external modem has a cable that connects it to your computer. It also has a cable that connects to a phone jack in the wall, plus a place for you to plug your desktop phone into the modem.

143

> ### Where to put Mr. PC
>
> The obvious place to set the computer is on a properly supported computer desk. You can set the computer's monitor on top of the computer box if you like, or set it to the side. (I prefer to the side since it keeps my head tilted down when I look at the screen, and that's good for the neck.)
>
> Avoid putting your computer in a spot where it can't breathe. Closed cupboards, cabinets, and closets make lousy computer homes. Computers need air to keep cool and need to be kept in a cool, relatively dry environment. Try not to set your computer in direct sunlight. In fact, setting a computer in front of a window is a bad idea since that's how most of them are stolen (via the old "smash-and-grab").
>
> Also, try to position the computer so that no lights shine directly into the monitor. That can really frazzle your eyes.

Turning it on

To use your computer, turn everything on! There once was a school of thought that said, "Turn the monitor on first, then the computer, then anything else, such as the printer." Then there was a different school (on the East Coast) that said, "Turn the computer box on last no matter what." So what gives?

The truth is, it really doesn't matter what goes on first. In fact, if you've invested in a power strip, just turn on everything and plug it into the strip. Then you can shut it all off with one switch (and do so with your toe — if you're that dexterous).

I actually had an experience once where my monitor would scream like it was scalded when I turned it on after I turned on the computer. Strange. However, when I turned the monitor on first, it didn't scream. If you experience some oddity like this, feel free to change the way you start your computer.

Turning it off

To turn off your computer, you just flip the various switches. If you have a power switch, just turn off its switch to shut everything down. That sounds easy, but there is a warning:

Never turn off your computer when a program is running! That means, always properly quit or exit your programs before you turn off the computer. On a PC, only turn it off when the screen says, "It's okay to turn off your computer" (or something similar), or you see the DOS prompt: C>.

The reason for this caution is that some computer programs leave pieces of themselves all over your hard drive if you just switch off the power without quitting first. Those pieces will slow down your computer's performance and lead to trouble later, so obey the rules and quit your programs before turning off the computer!

Breaking It In (the "Burn-In" Test)

One way to ensure that your new equipment is up-to-snuff is to put it through a special test. The object of this test is to break your new computer during the warranty period. If something is amiss, you want to know about it before the warranty expires.

When you first take your new computer home, follow these two instructions:

1. Keep your computer on 24 hours a day for two weeks.
2. Once a day, turn the machine off, wait a minute, and then turn it back on.

Because of the way electronic components are designed, faulty chips will usually go bad within the first 48 hours of use. By testing your computer this way, you'll be certain to find any faults immediately. Turning the power supply off and on each day helps to ensure that it is tough enough to stand the load.

After the two-week test, you can obey whatever on and off habits you've deemed proper for your computer. In fact, it will probably behave itself for years to come at that point!

Learning Your System

Give yourself time to read about your system, time to play, and time to relax and have fun with the computer. Believe it or not, the best way to learn about a computer system is to play around with it. Poke around. Test things. Try weird options and see what they do. As long as you're not rushed to start the serious work, you have time to easily grow with the system. Once the workload comes, you'll feel good about the system, and lo, that expected and much rumored frustration won't be there.

And here's another hint: After you've used your software for, say, a month, go back and re-read the manual. You'll be surprised at how much clearer it seems. It actually makes sense! (That's because people who write manuals are overly familiar with the product and forget what it's like to be a novice.)

By reading the manual a second time, you'll pick up a few more tips and learn some shortcuts by doing so. This is just another trick that the experts use to become experts.

✔ Quick Review

Set up your computer if someone hasn't done it for you. Plug everything into the wall, or into a power strip or UPS. Then turn it on!

You should run your system through a burn-in test for the first two weeks. Leave everything on all day, turning it off briefly once a day. This should "torture-test" the system and help you quickly find anything that's wrong while you're well within the warranty period.

Also, give yourself time to learn about your computer and your software. Feel free to play. There's nothing you can do to damage your computer, though don't use that as an excuse to be careless or not read instructions.

Enjoy your new computer!

APPENDIX A

Commonly Asked Questions

And Their Answers

Software

Q: What's the difference between a software's Version 1.2 and 1.3?

A: Version 1.3 lacks all the bugs that were found in Version 1.2. Likewise, when Version 1.4 comes out, it will have fixed all the bugs found in Version 1.3. Other improvements may come along the way as well, though they're usually presented in the major version releases, such as Version 1.4 up to 2.0.

Q: Is the "office suite" type of program considered integrated software?

A: No, it's more of a "bundled" software approach. You get several good programs all for one low price. Where they zing you is when it comes time to update; each program is updated individually, not as a whole like when you bought them.

Q: I don't have the manual because a friend gave me a copy of his disks.

A: This is theft. You should never use such software. You wouldn't think of going into the software store, taking the disks out of the package, and walking out the door without paying, would you? Also, this type of "freebie" is how computer viruses are spread.

Q: Should I worry about computer viruses?

A: Sadly, computer viruses are a fact of computing life. They are mischievous little programs that sneak onto your computer either to amuse, annoy, or curse you. Special programs called *virus utilities* can be used to check your system for signs of infection and remove the viruses. However, if you use only shrink-wrapped, store-bought software, you'll never have anything to worry about.

Microprocessors

Q: What's the difference between a 486SX and a 486DX?

A: The SX suffix causes a lot of confusion. This is because the old 386SX used only half the *bit width* of the 386DX. With a 486SX, all that's missing is the math coprocessor. So a 486SX running at 25MHz is just as fast as a 486DX running at the same speed. It only lacks the math coprocessor circuitry.

Q: What's the 2 mean in DX2 after a microprocessor's number?

A: It means the microprocessor is designed to run twice as fast, which is represented in its megahertz (MHz) number. So a 486DX2 running at 66MHz runs at 66MHz internally, but only 33MHz externally. This is only a technical point, nothing you should worry about. Always use the chip's advertised MHz speed for comparison.

Q: Which is faster, a 66MHz 486DX2 or a 66MHz 486DX?

A: The straight 66MHz 486DX will be faster. The DX2 runs at two speeds: Internally, it's 66MHz, but externally, it's only 33MHz. The full 486DX (no "2") runs at 66MHz both internally and externally.

APPENDIX A: COMMONLY ASKED QUESTIONS

Disk Drives

Q: Can I add a second floppy disk drive to my PC?

A: Yes. A good reason to do so is if you back up to floppy disks. Having two of them makes the process go a lot faster. Otherwise, most PCs only need one floppy drive.

Q: Can I add a second hard drive to my computer system?

A: Yes. Most PCs have room for two hard drives. If yours does, then you can add a second, larger hard drive quite easily, either by yourself or by having your dealer do it for you.

Monitors and Keyboards

Q: Will a bigger monitor display more colors?

A: No. It's not the monitor that's in charge of the colors; it's your video adapter card. You can plug the card into any size monitor, and it won't change how the card's circuitry displays colors. The only thing a bigger monitor gives you is a bigger image.

Q: My eyes hurt after computing. The wife says it's due to my computer's monitor. Is there anything I can do?

A: It's due more to the lights in the room than to your monitor. The lights will reflect off your computer screen, and that's what causes eye irritation. I'd recommend buying a nylon screen for your monitor. It cuts down on the glare and provides more contrast for a better image.

149

Q: Speaking of my wife, she says the computer will ruin my eyes. Is that true?

A: Not at all! Using your eyes does not cause them to go bad. Your eyes may become fatigued. When they do, get up and stare out a window for a while.

Printers and Peripherals

Q: How can I print 10-foot-long banners on my laser printer?

A: Banners are normally printed on dot matrix printers, which use continuous form-feed paper. On a laser printer, you usually print the banner a sheet at a time and then tape them together.

Q: My printer prints everything double-spaced. Help!

A: You need to throw a tiny switch inside the printer. Check your manual and find the switch labeled "Add LF to CR" or "Add linefeeds" or something similar. Turn it off. Conversely, if your printer prints everything all on one line, turn that same switch on.

Q: My PC's printer won't print at all.

A: You probably have two printer ports in your computer. There's nothing wrong with that, except that both ports are fighting over which one comes first. A PC can have up to four printers, named LPT1 through LPT4. You need to tell one of your printer ports that it's LPT2, and then everything will work fine.

Q: I can't afford an HP LaserJet, but I can buy an El-Cheapo laser printer with an HP emulator. The guy at the store says that it will work just like an HP, and I save about $700!

A: Avoid all forms of emulators unless you just want to tinker. You buy your hardware based on software. If your software wants an HP printer, buy it. Don't buy something-else-plus-an-emulator, even if it's cheaper.

Q: Can my CD player play music?

A: Sure, providing you have the proper multimedia software that lets your computer's CD-ROM drive play a musical CD.

Q: Can I hook up my fax machine to my computer?

A: Only if it's designed to do so.

Q: Will my computer receive faxes if it's turned off?

A: No, your computer won't do anything if it's turned off. It can receive faxes if you're not there, but you must have a fax/modem installed, and the software required to receive the fax must be running. External fax machines can receive faxes when the computer is off, but they must be on.

Computer Systems

Q: I want to write letters and balance my checkbook. Will a Pentium computer fill this need?

A: Fit the computer to meet your needs. Look for your checkbook balancing software *first*. Then match that software's lust for hardware, and that's how you'll tell what type of computer you'll need. This is the basic method this book offers. If, in the end, all indicators point to a Pentium, you can buy it.

Q: What's a "flash programmable BIOS"?

A: It's a special chip that can be upgraded without removing the computer's cover. The BIOS is your PC's personality chip, and often, manufacturers upgrade the BIOS to make it happier with newer PC components. In the olden days, you had to upgrade the chip by physically pulling out the old one and replacing it. With a flash BIOS, you can do the job by running a program on your computer. It makes upgrading simple.

Q: I want to buy one computer but hook up ten monitors and ten keyboards. Can I do that?

A: Not the way you think. What you really need is a file server and several workstations. One PC alone cannot manage such a feat, and certainly not for cheap.

Q: I'm interested in picking up a used computer system. How can I tell if it's any good?

A: First off, I don't recommend a used computer system if this is your first computer purchase. You're definitely cutting off your service and support, not to mention any warranty. For a second or third purchase, used computers are a deal; most of them still operate and are decent machines. Just take along some software to test-drive, and "kick the tires" by trying out the keyboard, monitor, and turning the unit on and off a few times.

Q: If a computer comes in green, can I get it in blue?

A: Computer colors are generally white, off-white, and beige. If there are any colors available, great. Otherwise, you'll have to spray-paint your system on your own and at your own risk.

General

Q: What does $CALL mean?

A: It means they can't print the price, either because the manufacturer won't let them or some other strange reason (such as, to foil the "we'll beat any advertised price" crowd). It may also be a ruse to get you to phone up the company to see how much the doojobbie costs. In fact, that's the "call" part of $CALL.

Q: Can I set my computer on the floor? Will it leave a grease spot?

A: The only important thing about setting a computer anywhere is giving it breathing space, as discussed in Chapter 15. Make sure that you don't set it on carpet that can clog any breathing slats. If you didn't buy a tower-style computer, consider getting a little stand to help stand your computer up on its side. And, no, there is no grease inside a computer to make a spot.

Q: My computer runs hot — sometimes it shuts itself off. What can I do?

A: Buy a new power supply or, better still, take your system into an authorized repair service.

Q: If I want to learn how to program my computer, where should I start?

A: Buy a book on programming. There are many excellent tutorials out there that let you work at your own pace. As far as a programming language is concerned, I'd recommend BASIC. Sounds easy enough.

Q: I want a question answered that hasn't been covered in this book. Where can I go for help?

A: First, try your dealer. You paid him money; he should give you the support and answer your question. He may redirect you to the software manufacturer if the problem is with your software. Second, try a local user group or a friend who is computer-knowledgeable. Third, you can also try writing away to those "Ask Dr. DOS" columnists in the national computer magazines. There is always help available for computers, and there are always people who are willing to help you.

APPENDIX **B**

Where to Find More Information

Some Places You Can Look

This book has taken you from knowing absolutely nothing about computers to becoming quite your own computer expert (computer literate, in fact). However, once you buy your own computer, you're going to need more information, such as how to use a particular piece of software or how to "manage" the information on your hard drive or even some suggestions or opinions about new trends and technology.

Fortunately, a wide variety of help is available, often from very knowledgeable people and occasionally for free. To boil it all down, there are three places where you can get more information about your computer:

- From computer magazines
- From computer books
- From user groups

Computer Magazines

Right away, you'll find out that there are few national computer magazines that will inform you on the same level as this book. There is a *Computer Novice* magazine, but I find its editorial material inconsistent. It drifts between being complex and overly patronizing, which isn't what you want. However, it's the best out there if you're just starting out. The other computer magazines assume you're already a computer expert, typically for a Fortune 500 company!

The bottom line is that you'll have to look. Plan on spending some time in the magazine section of a bookstore and find the best magazine for you. Find the magazine that's right up your alley and pick it up. At first, buy a bunch of them and then stick with the ones you wind up referring to the most. Use the prices in the ads to help you shop. Read the "tip" columns. Pay close attention to the reviews to help your buying decisions.

Computer Books

Computer books are very specific and usually only refer to one topic or one piece of software. Like magazines, they come in a variety of styles: some terse, some for the beginner, and some packed with a lot more information than any human could digest.

Topical computer books can help you with things like hard disk management, choosing software, working with software, or running your business using a number of computers. As with the magazines, look for a computer book that covers a topic or piece of software that you know.

Since the early '80s, public libraries have grown sensitive to the needs of computer users and now have good selections of computer trade books. (This beats the old days when they stocked only technical books.) You might consider going to the library and browsing through a few books to see what you like best. If you find a handy reference, buy it at the bookstore and keep it near your computer.

Computer User Groups

One of the best parts of the computer age is that people just like you — all types of folk — who own the same computer get together regularly to exchange ideas, chat, and answer questions regarding computing. These people are called "users," and their organizations are called "user groups."

Appendix B: Where to Find More Information

You'll find user groups listed in the newspaper or a local computer magazine or flier. These sources will list meeting times, a contact person, and most importantly, the group's focus. For example, there may be a group on the Harvard Graphics program, and you've been having trouble with the program. If so, stop by the user group meeting and ask some questions. You'll walk away knowing more about your software, and maybe even make a few computer friends. (That last thought frightened me when I first went to a user group meeting, but I eventually found out computer people are just as normal as everyone else.)

The best user groups will offer you buying tips and suggestions that you can't get from your dealer. They may also have presentations and demonstrations where you can learn more about your PC and its software. After a while, you may find yourself showing up just to have fun. You might even start answering others' questions after a time.

Glossary and Index

■■■■■■■■■■■■■■■■■■■■■■■■■■■■■

$CALL, *153*

The price is too low to print. Call us and find out how much we want for it.

286, *50*

A short term for the 80286 microprocessor chip. See *80286*.

2x, *115*

A speed rating for a CD-ROM drive, meaning the drive is twice as fast as a slow, music-playing CD player. Refer to *data transfer rate*.

386, 386DX, 386SX, *150*

Various abbreviations for the 80386 microprocessor chip. See *80386*.

3x, *115*

A speed rating for a CD-ROM drive, which is three times faster than the old, el-sluggo drives. See *data transfer rate*.

486, *49–50*

A term for the fourth-generation microprocessor chip available in IBM-compatible computers. It may also be called an 80486 or i486.

586, *49–50*

See *Pentium*.

80286, *50*

The second-generation microprocessor available in IBM PC/AT and similar models. This processor was replaced by the 80386 chip in the mid-80s. Today, you'll only find it in used computers.

80386, *49–50*

The third-generation microprocessor available to IBM-compatible computers or "PCs." This chip succeeded the 80286 microprocessor. It's also called the 80386DX, 386, and 386DX. The 386SX (or 80386SX) chip is a cheaper, not-as-powerful version, often found in laptop computers.

80x86, *47–55*

A shortcut name for a microprocessor in just about any PC or IBM-compatible computer. The *x* is replaced with another numeral, such as a 2, 3, or 4. This just means the microprocessor is a general, Intel-type, PC microprocessor. Nothing special.

8514, 8514/a, *76*

A PC graphics standard superior to *VGA* and similar to *SVGA*.

access time, *67, 115*

The way that a hard drive's speed is measured. Each hard drive has a different access time, measured in milliseconds. The fewer the milliseconds, the faster the hard drive.

Alpha-Bits™, *59*

A cold breakfast cereal composed of letter-shaped nuggets, ala alphabet soup. Spelling your name in your spoon with Alpha-Bits cereal is the equivalent of winning the Nobel Prize among eight-year-olds.

Analog-to-Digital (A-to-D), *86, 89*

Another term for your computer's *joystick port*. It's called Analog-to-Digital because it translates the smooth, real-world movements of the joystick into the digital ones and zeros that the computer can digest.

applications software, *15*

Computer software for the Apple and Macintosh computers is often referred to as applications software. See *software*.

Baud, *112*

A communications term. Baud is used interchangeably, though incorrectly, with BPS (see *BPS*). The word is derived from J.M.E. Baudot, a 19th-century French inventor and telegrapher.

benchmark, 53
A gauge of how fast a computer is, or how efficiently it performs some task. Computer ads boast of benchmark tests, and computer magazines run batteries of tests to figure out which PC is fastest. These tests rarely have any bearing on how your computer performs, though they can be used for comparison purposes. See the box, "My computer's faster than yours! Nya! Nya! Nya!" in Chapter 6 for more information.

binary, 60-61
A counting base (from the Latin *bi*) with only two elements. Computers count using the values 0 and 1, thereby using the binary number system, also referred to as Base Two.

BIOS, 21
The primary instructions that get a computer up in the morning. BIOS (*BYE-oss*) stands for Basic Input/Output System, and its information is stored in a special chip inside the computer. BIOS's primary job is to get the computer started and then load DOS from disk. See *ROM*.

bit, 61
Contraction of BInary digiT. A bit is a binary number and has the value 1 and 0 representing on and off. In microcomputers, bits are grouped into sets of eight, called a *byte*.

bit width, 50, 61
The number of bits a microprocessor can digest at a time. The more bits — or the "wider" the bit width — the more powerful the microprocessor. Common bit widths are 8, 16, 32, and 64. The bigger, the better.

boat anchor, 17
A derogatory term for a useless computer, typically brought about because the computer has no software that makes it worth its weight. Other terms include *doorstop, paper weight, foot stool*, or anything that is large and unmoving.

boot
To start a computer.

boot disk
A disk you use to start your computer.

BPS, 111–112

An acronym for bits per second; it's the total number of bits transmitted during one second. *Baud* is commonly mistaken to mean BPS; however, BPS is correct for microcomputer communications.

bundled software, 44

Several programs that carry out different tasks, all stuffed into one box. You can buy them all separately for more money, or together in a "suite" to save some dollars. Note that this is not *bungled* software.

bus, 94

Another term for a computer's *expansion slot*. Specifically, it's not only the slot, but also the electronics and protocols used for communications between any *expansion card* and the computer's microprocessor.

byte, 59–60

A storage unit for information in a computer. Technically, a byte is a group of eight *bits*. Big deal! Think of a byte instead as a cubbyhole in which your computer stores a piece of information, such as a character or letter of the alphabet. Bytes are used en masse to store lots of information. See *kilobyte* and *megabyte*.

cache, 54–55

A storage place in memory, typically used to speed something up. A microprocessor's cache speeds it up; a disk cache program can speed up your disk drives. Pronounce it *cash*.

Central Processing Unit, 47

See *microprocessor*.

Centronics port, 86–87

A nerdy term for a *printer port*.

CGA

An acronym for Color Graphic Adapter, a common color adapter for the early IBM PC and clones. It was supplanted by the EGA graphics standard.

clone
One of a variety of brands of computers, all modeled after one original. A clone computer behaves similarly to and runs the same programs as the original, although it's usually much cheaper. Back in the early days, all PCs modeled after the original IBM PC were known as clones. Today, the term has fallen by the wayside, though a few old fogies may still use it.

closed architecture
A kind of computer that has no expansion options. A closed architecture computer is sold as a complete box. There are no "slots" inside a closed architecture computer, nor are there any upgrade paths.

command-driven
Software that you control by typing in commands. This is usually harder than *menu-driven* software because you must know the commands in advance; they're not visible on-screen and easily selectable from a menu. This type of software does have the advantage of being quick to use once you know the commands.

compatible
Refers to how well things get along, whether they're two programs, computers, hardware and software, software and an operating system, and so on. When software (or whatever) isn't compatible with your stuff, then it won't work, and you'll be sore with disappointment.

compatibility, 18
The ability to take hardware and software designed for another kind of computer and run it on your own. If it works, then you're compatible. The highest levels of incompatibility are found in computer games. Games written for one kind of computer won't work on a non-compatible computer.

compiler, 41
A software program that creates other software programs. The compiler is the main part of a programming language package, such as C/C++ or the BASIC programming language.

composite
A cheap kind of monitor offered as a compromise between expensive color and graphic-less monochrome for the early PC user. Composite monitors could display graphics and "colors" in shades of gray, but the quality of text and graphics was very poor.

computer, 8
A device that's highly useful and can be easily understood. Given that, keep in mind that you'll eventually, and perhaps, unfortunately, often find them highly frustrating companions.

console
As a noun, it means the box part of your computer; the thing that houses the disk drives, memory, microprocessor, and other electronic goodies. It may also refer to the keyboard and monitor as well. See *system unit*. As a verb, it refers to what you do to a friend who has made an unwise computer purchase.

conventional memory, 62
The first 640K of memory in your computer. This memory is used by DOS programs, which may claim, "I require 550K of conventional memory." Most computers today are sold with 640K of conventional memory, which means they'll run any old DOS program, no sweat.

CPS, 102
Acronym for characters per second, the number of characters a dot matrix printer can spit out in one second. This is a comparison figure used to rate different printers' speed.

CPU, 47
An acronym for Central Processing Unit. See *microprocessor*.

CRT, 75–80
An acronym for Cathode Ray Tube, what a sophomore computer science student would call a computer's *monitor*.

cursor, 91
A solid block or flashing underline on the computer screen. Characters typed at the keyboard or displayed by the computer appear at the cursor's position. It's from the Latin word for "runner."

data

Information, not necessarily text characters, used by a computer. Most every program uses data that you can input or read from a disk file. Pronounce it DAY-tuh.

database, 16, 36

A program used for storing information. The information in a database can be printed, sorted, searched, and manipulated in a variety of ways.

data transfer rate, 115

A measure of a CD-ROM drive's speed, it refers to the number of kilobytes the drive can cough up per second. A speed of 150K per second is slow, 300K per second is about right, and 450K per second means you paid a lot for your drive and are enjoying superb performance.

density, 71-72

Refers to the amount of information that can be packed onto a disk. Floppy disks are measured in single, double, high, and extended densities.

desktop

Can refer to the top of your desk. (Like, duh!) Also refers to the computer screen background when you're running a special type of graphical operating system, such as *Windows*.

desktop PC, 11

A computer designed to sit on top of your desk, as opposed to a *laptop* computer or a larger computer.

desktop publishing, 35

A type of software that lets you combine words and pictures (usually created separately) into one package. You can use desktop publishing to create anything from leaflets to pamphlets to brochures to even something as ambitious as a book. (This book was created using such a package.) Beware that *desktop publishing* is often abbreviated as DP.

diagnostic software, 39-40

Special programs that will tell you what's in your computer or what's wrong with your computer.

disk
A recording medium for computer storage. There are three kinds of disks: 5¼-inch floppy diskettes, 3½-inch diskettes, and hard disks.

diskette
Another term for a disk. Diskette usually applies to any type of flexible media, that is, a floppy diskette.

display
Something shown or visible on the computer's monitor. Display also refers to the computer screen, whereas monitor refers to the box around the screen.

DOS, 22-23
An acronym for Disk Operating System; rhymes with "boss." The series of programs that controls the computer's interaction with humans and parts of the computer. DOS also controls the disk drive and loads, saves, and executes programs. DOS is the computer's manager.

DOS prompt
A place on-screen where you type DOS commands. It usually looks like this: C>. And it's followed by a blinking underline or *cursor*. After typing your command at the DOS prompt, press Enter to send the command to DOS for processing, or instant ridicule if you've made even the tiniest mistake.

dot matrix, 100
A type of printer that produces its output by stabbing little pins at a ribbon to produce a pattern of dots on the paper. Hopefully, the pattern of dots resembles letters that humans can recognize.

dot pitch, 79
The size of the tiny dots that form an image on your monitor's screen, measured in millimeters. The smaller the dot pitch, the finer the resolution on the monitor.

download
A *modem* term that refers to the process of copying a file or software from another computer to your computer. You need a modem and communications software to make this happen. (*Uploading* is the process of sending a file to another computer using your modem.)

drawing, 37
Software used to create illustrations, preferably mechanical drawings, or "line art." See *painting*.

DS/DD, 72
An abbreviation for a double-sided, double-density floppy disk. These diskettes were popular from about 1981 through 1992, when they were replaced by the high capacity $3^1/_2$-inch diskettes.

dump
Inelegant computer jargon for a transfer of information, such as the contents of the screen, memory, or data in a file, to another place. For example, copying the characters on-screen to a printer is called a "screen dump."

DX, 50-52
A suffix on some microprocessor names. Alone, it means "the whole enchilada," or the true microprocessor and not some SX 16/32 hybrid. When followed by a number, it means that the microprocessor has double (or triple or quadruple) speed internally.

ECP/EPP, 86-87
Acronym for Enhanced Capabilities Port/Enhanced Parallel Port. It's a type of super printer port.

EGA
An acronym for Enhanced Graphics Adapter. A high resolution, multi-color graphics card for the IBM PC and clones. EGA was supplanted by the VGA standard in 1987.

el queso grande, 17
Spanish: The Big Cheese. Leader.

emulation
The ability of one piece of hardware (computer, printer, modem, and so on) to fake the characteristics of another.

emulator
A piece of hardware that performs emulation. Hardware emulators are the cheapest and worst ways to tweak the performance of one computer out of another. If you want to run software on a particular computer, buy that computer! If you need one type of printer, buy it! Do not buy a cheaper piece of hardware with an emulator and expect to get the job done.

ergonomic, 82

Something designed so people can use it, as opposed to something designed for the heck of it, which is usually uncomfortable. For example, an ergonomic computer mouse would fit comfortably in the palm of your hand. A non-ergonomic mouse would be shaped like a Jell-O mold.

execute

Another term for starting a program. See *run*. It may also refer to carrying out some task. Execute is a popular term with computer people, primarily because one of its definitions is "to put to death."

expanded memory, 62

Excess memory used by DOS programs. A 1MB 386 or later computer has about 348K of expanded memory. Typically, a special program is used to configure your computer's normal memory (called *extended memory*) into expanded memory.

expansion card, 93

A printed circuit board that is added to your computer. An expansion card allows you to add optional features to your computer. If you're good with tinker-toys, you can do this one yourself.

expansion slot, 93, 110

A slot inside the computer (on the motherboard) where a variety of optional expansion cards are plugged. See *expansion cards*.

extended memory, 62

Any memory in excess of 1MB on a 386 or later computer. For example, if you buy a 486 computer with 4MB of memory, you'll have 3MB of extended memory.

file

A collection of information on disk. A file can contain text characters, binary information, or programming instructions.

fixed disk, 67

See *hard disk*.

floating point unit, 53

Another name for a *math coprocessor*. Specifically, it's a math coprocessor built into a microprocessor, which is what you'll find in a 486DX or Pentium.

floppy diskette, 70, 73
A $5^1/_4$-inch or $3^1/_2$-inch diskette used for recording programs, data files, and text files. The floppy diskette is a permanent kind of storage. The information stays on diskette until it's erased.

footprint
The size your computer box takes up on your desktop. Early PCs were huge, taking up almost three square feet! Today's computers are smaller, which they call "small footprint" computers.

format, 72
A way of preparing a disk to be used for storing information. Formatting organizes a disk, arranging it so a computer can access the disk, read from it, and write to it. All disks must be formatted by your computer and your operating system before they can be used.

f.p.u., 53
See *floating point unit*.

gigabyte, 68
One billion bytes, one thousand megabytes, or one million K. It's abbreviated G or GB and often pronounced "gig" at trendy Rodeo Drive computer boutiques.

graphics, 76-78
The ability of a computer to draw and display lines, circles, boxes, and other interesting shapes in various colors on-screen. A computer without graphics capabilities can display only text characters. A computer with graphics capabilities is much more expensive.

graphics accelerator
Either software or hardware designed to make your PC's graphics go very fast. This is a must for anyone who uses graphical applications.

graphics adapter, 76
Same thing as *graphics card*.

graphics card, 76
The *controller* inside your PC that controls the graphics, text, colors, and other things that appear on-screen.

graphics standard
One of several three letter acronyms that describes the color and graphics resolution for a PC graphics card. Standards include VGA, SVGA, XGA, EGA, CGA, and la-di-da.

guarantee, 122-124
A promise to fully replace or repair a defective something at absolutely no cost to you. If you must pay for labor, then what you have is a *warranty*.

GUI
Acronym for Graphical User Interface, a type of program that uses graphics and other fun stuff to communicate with you instead of terse text. If done right, it can make using a computer easier. GUI is often pronounced *gooey*, though I think that's quite dumb.

hacker
A computer whiz — someone who is familiar with the inner workings of a computer and loves to fiddle in a mechanical or programming way. Anyone who's enthused about computers can be considered a hacker.

hard copy, 8, 97
A term for printed information produced by a computer (the computer's printer). Also, a sleazy tabloid TV show.

hard disk, 66-67, 133
This term refers to the disk located inside a hard drive, often used interchangeably with *hard drive*. The reason there are two terms is that with a floppy disk you have both the disk (which you can take out) and the drive (which is part of the computer). A hard disk is a permanent part of a hard drive, which confuses people, so they use either term to refer to the same thing.

hard drive, 8, 67, 133
A non-removable type of storage for your computer programs and files. A hard drive accesses information quickly and is capable of storing much more information than a floppy disk. Hard drives are a must for almost every application available today. They're fast, efficient, and relatively inexpensive.

hard drive controller, 69-70
The piece of electronics that controls the hard drive (duh!). It's responsible for connecting the hard drive to the computer's main circuitry board and, therefore, to the microprocessor. There are two popular styles of hard drive controller: IDE and SCSI.

hardware, 8
The physical parts of a computer: the motherboard or computer itself, disk drives, monitor, printer, modem, and so on. Hardware is anything you can bang on, so to speak.

high capacity disks, 72
Floppy disks capable of storing a lot of information, more than the old DS/DD diskettes. A 3$^1/_2$-inch high capacity diskette stores 1.44MB of information; a 5$^1/_4$-inch high capacity diskette stores 1.2MB.

high density disks, 72
Another term for high capacity disks.

IDE, 69
An acronym for Integrated Drive Electronics, a type of hard disk controller for a PC.

ink jet printer, 103-104
A special kind of printer that actually squirts ink onto the page. Ink jet printers need no ribbons. Because they spray ink directly onto the page, they can "paint" graphics nicely. They're quiet, too.

InPort, 86, 89
Microsoft's pet name for its mouse port.

input
Information given to the computer, such as information typed at the keyboard. The computer chews on this, thinks it over, and then hopefully produces the right kind of output.

integrated software, 7, 44-45
One single software package that carries out a number of tasks. For example, one program that serves as a word processor, spreadsheet, database, and communications program. See *bundled software*.

interlacing, 79
A method by which a monitor's electron gun "paints" information on a computer screen. Non-interlaced monitors only paint the information once, which makes them easier on the eyes.

Internet, 38
A vast network of computers that shares information and provides various services. Just about anyone can dial into the Internet service to access the information; special software is provided to let you do this, plus you must pay a fee to the company that provides you Internet access.

I/O
An abbreviation for Input/Output. An I/O device is one capable of both sending (output) and receiving (input) information.

jack
Refers to a connector, plug, or hole into which the connector or plug plugs into. Can also mean *nothing,* as in, "He doesn't know jack."

joystick, 86, 89-90
A kanobbie you use to play games with.

joystick port, 86, 89-90
The hole in the back of your computer where the joystick plugs in.

K, 60
An abbreviation for kilobyte. 1K stands for 1 kilobyte, 64K stands for 64 kilobytes. A K, or kilobyte, is equal to 1,024 bytes.

K5
A Pentium-compatible microprocessor. The K stands for Krypton, which is an in-joke. AMD, manufacturer of the K5, plans on using it to "kill" Intel and its Pentium processor. Intel is Superman, and Kryptonite is the only substance that makes him wimpy.

keyboard, 80-82
Humans speak to computers by typing on the keyboard. It's a flat panel of buttons that you press to talk to your computer.

kilobyte, 60
One kilobyte has 1,024 bytes of information. Kilo means 1,000 of something. In computers, "K" stands for 1,024 because it's the closest power of two to 1,000. (Computers love their twos tables.)

laptop computer, 11
A special type of portable computer designed to be lightweight and run off batteries. The laptop computer contains just about everything a desktop PC has.

laser printer, 104–105
A special kind of printer that works like a copying machine. Text printed on a laser printer is near-typeset quality. They're a wee-bit expensive for the home, yet ideal in office situations.

launch
Yet another term used for running a program on your computer. This one is more elegant and elitist than *run*.

load
A transfer of information, such as a text file or program, from disk to computer memory.

local bus, 95
A type of *expansion slot* in a PC that accommodates a video adapter (for graphics), hard drive, or some other device that demands a lot of the microprocessor's attention. The local bus is essentially a very fast *expansion slot,* communicating with the microprocessor almost directly.

Luddite
Someone who is afraid of new technology, or one who is so opposed to technology as to proclaim that it's evil. The term comes from Ned Ludd, one of many English workmen in the 19th century who, as a form of protest, destroyed machines designed to ease drudgery.

M, MB, 59, 133
An abbreviation for megabyte. See *megabyte*.

M1
A Pentium-compatible microprocessor from Cyrix.

mainframe (computer)
A large, central computer that serves from several dozen to hundreds of people.

math coprocessor, 51-52
A companion chip for the microprocessor, one that does mathematical operations very fast. The 486 (but not 486SX) and *Pentium* microprocessors have their own built-in math coprocessor. Older chips must buy and install one separately.

megabyte, 60, 133
One million bytes, or one thousand *K*. This used to be a lot of memory, but nowadays, it's fairly common. See *kilobyte*.

megahertz, 51
The speed of a microprocessor. *Mega* means million, and *Hertz* is a rental car company. Seriously, hertz refers to the number of cycles per second, or the number of times something repeats in one second. So 50 megahertz means a microprocessor whizzes along at 50 million cycles per second — fast.

memory, 8, 133
A place where programs, characters, graphics, or almost everything inside a computer is stored. Computer memory is erased when the computer is turned off. Also see *RAM*.

memory manager, 62
A special computer program, or utility, that oversees memory and grants access when your programs beg for it.

menu-driven
A piece of software that has its commands displayed in a menu. Supposedly, this makes the software easier to use because you can view the commands and pick the one you want. The advantage here is that the program is easy to learn because you can see the commands on the menu. The opposite type of software is called *command-driven*.

MHz, 51
An abbreviation for megahertz. See *megahertz*.

microcomputer
The term for a desktop computer or *PC* in the early years. It's actually a put-down, since not much was thought of them in the early days. The name also refers to the computer's main chip, the *microprocessor*. Today, these computers are called *desktop* computers or just *PCs*.

microprocessor, 17–18
A special computer chip; the computer's main chip. Its own calculator, the chip that does all the thinking. All other elements of the computer are controlled by the microprocessor. It might also be called the *CPU,* for Central Processing Unit, or just the *processor*.

Microsoft
A large software company based in Redmond, Washington. The company originally marketed the definitive microcomputer programming language, BASIC. It later went on to write MS-DOS, Windows, and several other popular programs. Microsoft's ultimate goal is to eventually write the software that runs the universe.

MIDI, 90
An acronym for Musical Instrument Digital Interface. It's a port into which you can plug synthesizer keyboards and other musical instruments for composing music with a personal computer.

millisecond
One-thousandth of a second, abbreviated *ms*.

mini-computer
A medium-sized computer, not as big as a *mainframe* and not a desktop computer. These computers were used by colleges and small businesses that couldn't afford mainframe computers. Most of today's expensive desktop computers would be considered *mini-computers* a few decades ago.

mini-tower
A squat version of a tower PC, often designed to sit on your desktop instead of the floor.

modem, 38, 109–113
A device used to let your computer talk to other computers over the phone. The term is a contraction of MOdulator-DEModulator, in case you were curious.

monitor, 75
The computer display — that TV thing on which you see information displayed by the computer. Note that the monitor refers to the whole box. The term *screen* means the front, or glass part, on which you see information.

monochrome
A type of computer monitor that displays only one "color" and black, such as the classic green text on a black background.

motherboard
A fiberglass sheet containing the computer's microprocessor, microchips, and other electronics. A motherboard is a computer's main piece of circuitry.

mouse, 91, 86–89
A palm-sized device used for interacting with a program. The mouse moves a *mouse pointer* on-screen, and that movement can be used to control various aspects of a program.

mouse pointer, 91
The graphical doodad on your computer screen that mimics the movements of the computer mouse on your desktop. It may also be referred to as a *cursor*.

ms
An abbreviation for millisecond, often used in lower case, as in 20 ms. See *millisecond*.

MS-DOS
The version of DOS marketed by Microsoft. MS-DOS stands for the Microsoft Disk Operating System.

multimedia, 41–42
A term for a computer capable of playing music, animation, video, and a bunch of other "fun" things. A multimedia PC is typically equipped with a *sound card* and CD-ROM drive.

network
A series of individual computers all connected to one another in order to exchange information. A common phrase in computer usage is "Does your NETWORK?"

NI, 79
Abbreviation identifying a non-interlaced monitor. See *interlacing*.

NLQ, 101
An abbreviation for near letter quality. It's high-quality output from a *dot matrix* printer that looks like it was produced by a typewriter or laser printer.

ns
An abbreviation for nanosecond, one-billionth of a second — very fast. Computer memory is often measured in nanoseconds.

OCR
An acronym for Optical Character Recognition, a type of software that uses a computer scanner to read in text from a book or piece of paper. Sometimes it actually works.

on-line service, 38
A company that provides a place for you to call with your modem, letting you do interesting things. Major on-line services include CompuServe, Prodigy, America Online, GEnie, and a host of others. Local systems, usually run by hobbyists, are referred to as *BBSs*, for Bulletin Board Systems.

open
To take a file or document on disk and load it into an application so you can work on it. You open files previously saved to disk. To work on that nasty letter in your word processor, you *open* it.

open architecture, 93
A kind of computer that has expansion slots or other methods of allowing you to expand and configure your own system.

177

operating system, 9

The program that runs the computer, controlling interaction between a computer's operator (meaning you), the hardware, and the software. The operating system is your most important piece of software. Refer to *DOS, Windows, UNIX,* and *OS/2.*

orphan

A computer whose manufacturer has gone out of business. The computer industry is riddled with these computers; they may be technologically powerful, but since the company that made them went belly-up, the computers are *orphans,* and their owners live without any warranty, technical support, or hopeful future. Yes, it's dismal.

OS/2, 22-23

The second-generation operating system from IBM and Microsoft, designed to supplant DOS. It stands for Operating System Two, and it's pronounced Oh-Ess-Too. OS/2 was introduced back in 1987. Since then, OS/2 has become a niche operating system, albeit a powerful one with many admirers. (See Chapter 3 for a discussion of OS/2.)

output

What the computer produces. This is information you see displayed on-screen or printed on the printer. See *input.*

OverDrive chip

A microprocessor upgrade. Such upgrades could give your 486SX chip full 486DX power.

P-something

Some microprocessors from Intel Corporation are dubbed the P-this or P-that before they're given specific names. The Pentium was originally the P5. The next generation microprocessor is dubbed the P6.

painting, 37

Software used to make pictures. This contrasts with drawing programs in that the painting is more free-hand, like real painting. Drawing software is more precise.

parallel
Refers to the way data is sent with bits side-by-side, rather than one after the other (serial). Compare parallel to people in a parade, marching eight-abreast. Serial is single-file.

parallel port, 86–87
Another term for the *printer port*.

PC, 141–146
An acronym for personal computer, though it's come to mean any computer that's compatible with the original IBM PC, or can run the DOS or Windows operating system. Even so, the Macintosh and other computers can be called a *PC* because they're personal computers (one computer for one person as opposed to *mainframe* or *mini-computers*).

PC-DOS
The disk operating system for the IBM PC and family. PC-DOS is licensed to IBM from Microsoft, which also markets its own version of the operating system called MS-DOS.

PCI, 95
A type of local bus port. It stands for Peripheral Component Interconnect. This is the most popular type of local bus, the one I recommend. See *local bus*.

PCMCIA
PCMCIA stands for Personal Computer Memory Card International Association. It refers to an expansion slot and a type of card on some PC laptops. I would guess that it's pronounced letters-only, though there may be some other cute way to pronounce it that I haven't yet heard.

Pentium, 49–50
The name given to the fifth-generation microprocessor found in IBM-compatible computers. Its name was chosen by Intel because they couldn't get a trademark for the numbers 586.

peripheral, 8, 73, 109
A device external to the computer, such as a printer, modem, monitor, and so on. It can also refer to various items you buy after you buy the main computer "box."

personal computer, 141-146
See *PC*.

pixel, 77
Contraction of PICture ELement, it's a dot on the computer's screen. The number of pixels that can be generated determine the resolution of graphics on the computer. A computer with a resolution of 640 pixels across and 200 pixels down has a grid of 128,000 dots on which to plot graphics.

port, 85, 143
A port is a "hole in the back of the computer." Into these ports are plugged a variety of devices that communicate with the computer. See *printer port* and *serial port*.

power bar, 118
Another term for a *power strip*.

power protector, 118, 142
A device you plug your PC into that suppresses some of the nasty electrical things that can damage your computer's delicate innards.

power strip, 118, 142
A cheap electrical outlet extender that doesn't really offer much protection but does give you more than one socket to help plug in your PC's peripherals.

p.p.m., 105
An abbreviation for pages per minute, the speed at which laser printers are judged and compared.

printer, 8, 86, 97
A device that prints characters on paper, like a typewriter. Refer to Chapter 11.

printer driver, 106
A special piece of software that controls your printer. This is usually a part of another application. For example, your word processor should come with a printer driver that supports your printer. Without it, you won't be able to use all your printer's cool features.

printer port, 86–87
The "hole in the back of the computer" that the printer plugs into. Information is sent to the printer via the printer port. It's also known as a *parallel port* and occasionally called a *Centronics port*.

processor, 47
See *microprocessor*.

prompt
A single character used to ask for entry of a command or line of text. A prompt is used when a computer program is asking you to input information. It has nothing to do with being on time.

proprietary, 115
Something with only one owner or something with a single standard, not compatible with anything else. Try to avoid proprietary stuff when you buy computer peripherals. Keep with the standards.

public domain, 27, 43
A free program. Software donated to the public domain can be copied and used without charge. See *shareware*.

RAID
Acronym for Redundant Array of Inexpensive Disks. It refers to a stack of hard drives used to ensure that information is never lost, typically on a large computer such as a *file server*.

RAM, 47, 57, 133
An acronym for Random Access Memory. See *memory*.

Random Access Memory, 47, 57, 133
Computer memory. The random aspect means the memory can be written to and read from. This type of memory is often called *RAM* or just *memory*.

Read-Only Memory, 21
Computer memory that can be read (like *Random Access Memory*) but cannot be written to or altered. It's "read-only," and therefore, it never changes or loses its information when the computer is turned off.

redundant
See *redundant*.

release number, 147
A number given computer software to let you know how up-to-date it is. The first release number or *version* is usually 1.0. Minor updates follow as release numbers 1.1, 1.2, and so on. The next major update is numbered 2.0, followed by minor updates 2.1, 2.2, and so on. The higher the release number, the longer the software has been around.

ROM, 21
An acronym of Read-Only Memory. Some strange computers may also call ROM *firmware*. See *Read-Only Memory*.

RS-232, 86-88
What burned-out computer users may call the serial port. (RS-232 equals serial port.) It's an acronym of Required Standard 232 of the Electronics Industry Association.

run
To start a program. It may also refer to the state where your computer is on and working properly — that is, *running*.

save
To transfer data from memory to disk. When you save a program, you are making a permanent recording of it on disk. See *load*.

scanner, 118
A peripheral device that reads an image into the computer, similar to the way a copy machine reads an image.

screen saver
A program that "blanks" the screen, preventing an image to be "burned" on the phosphor. Screen saver programs work after a period of time. For example, if you don't type anything on the keyboard for several minutes, the screen blanks or is filled with a random (and often humorous) pattern.

SCSI, 69-70, 85-86, 90-91

A Small Computer System Interface port, like an ultra-fast serial port. The SCSI ("scuzzy") port allows you to connect a variety of devices to your computer: a hard drive, printer, optical disk, scanner, and so on. Using only one SCSI port, you can "chain" all your SCSI devices together. Neat-o.

serial, 86-88

Refers to the way data is sent with bits following one after another, as opposed to parallel, where bits are sent side-by-side. Serial has nothing to do with breakfast.

serial mouse, 89

A type of computer mouse that plugs into one of your computer's *serial ports*. See *mouse*.

serial port, 86-88, 110

A port that enables a computer to have two-way communication with a peripheral device or with another computer. Two popular items to plug into your PC's serial port are a modem and a computer mouse.

shareware, 43

These programs are just like *public domain* except the author requests a donation if you use and enjoy the software. This is typically accomplished through a series of "guilt messages" before or after the program runs.

shell program

A special type of *utility* program that makes working with your computer and files on disk a lot easier. The shell presents information in a plain, friendly manner. Supposedly a shell program won't intimidate you as much as DOS or however your computer normally deals with files.

shrink wrap

The Saran Wrap-like plastic used to enclose computer software and other off-the-shelf products.

software, 15

Programming instructions for a computer. Software is a set of instructions that tells the computer what to do. Though software comes on a disk, it is the actual magnetically encoded instructions on the disk and not the disk itself that make up the software.

software base, 18
Refers to the number of programs available for your computer. The larger the software base, the more variety and choice you have in the programs you can run on your computer.

sound card, 114
A PC expansion card that allows your computer to play music, synthesize its own music, generate human speech, or play recorded speech. This is a key element in creating a multimedia PC.

spreadsheet, 34-35
Software used to manipulate numbers, like a gigantic calculator, though most modern spreadsheets are capable of a lot more than just "crunching" numbers. Spreadsheets are one of the most popular pieces of business software.

SS/DD, 71
An abbreviation for a single-sided, double-density floppy disk. SS/DD disks typically hold up to 180K of information.

SS/SD, 71
An abbreviation for a single-sided, single-density floppy disk. SS/SD disks typically hold up to 100K of information.

start
To begin a program; another term for *run*.

surge suppresser, 118-119, 142
A type of *power strip* that also has some capabilities to protect your computer from the evils of your power company, specifically power surges. For more money, you can buy a surge suppresser that also protects against spikes, sags, and even blackouts (called a *UPS*).

SVGA, 76
An acronym for SuperVGA or Super Video Graphics Array, the PC graphics standard that superseded the old VGA standard. It's just a wee bit better but worth every penny.

system unit
The nerdy, techy term that refers to the box where your computer's disk drives, memory, microprocessor, and other pieces parts live. Personally, I prefer the term *console*.

text editor, 40
A type of word processor used primarily for writing down words — just plain text. Text editors lack fancy text formatting and printing abilities. They're primarily used to edit text files on disk, such as DOS's AUTOEXEC.BAT file, or when programming a computer.

tower PC
A type of desktop computer that sits on its side in an up-and-down configuration. Usually, these behemoths squat on the floor under your desk. They have a lot more room inside than standard desktop computer models.

UART, 86-88
Pronounced YOO-art, it's the main chip in your PC's *serial port*.

UNIX, 22-23
An operating system from AT&T, found normally on minicomputers, though a version exists for PCs, as well. It's very advanced and lacks the software available to DOS, so forget any chance of working with UNIX in the near future.

upgrade, 131
To replace or improve a piece of hardware or software. You upgrade hardware by replacing it with a newer, larger, faster piece of hardware. You can also improve some hardware by adding options to it: more memory, a second disk drive, another microprocessor, and so on. Software is upgraded by replacing the old version with a newer version.

UPS, 118-119, 142
Acronym for Uninterruptible Power Supply (or Source). A device that lets you run your computer during brief blackouts and also protects the system from electrical nasties.

user groups, 125
A rag-tag collection of computer users who gather once every so often to talk computers. These non-profit groups are open to everyone, though they usually target a specific computer or piece of software. Keep in mind that they aren't "expert-only," though often many experts are there who are more than willing to share their advice. Refer to your newspaper or computer flier for a list of groups, meeting times, and places.

user interface
The way a program is designed to interact with a user. Some nice computers, such as the Macintosh, have a friendly, graphics-oriented user interface. Other computers have an unfriendly, command-line interface.

utility, 39–40
A type of software that carries out repair, diagnostic, or performance-enhancing tasks.

version, 147
Refers to the release number of computer software. See *release number*.

VESA, 95
A type of local bus port. It stands for Video Electronics Standards Association and was introduced primarily to give PCs very fast video. It can, however, be used to add other devices to a computer as well. See *local bus*.

VGA, 76
A graphics standard introduced with the IBM PS/2 series of computers. VGA, pronounced vee-jee-ay, stands for Video Graphics Array.

video board, 76
See *graphics card*.

video memory, 144
Special memory (RAM) used only by your PC's video. The more video memory you have, the better your PC's graphics will be.

Video RAM, 133
Same thing as *video memory*.

VL-bus, 95
An abbreviation for VESA-local bus port. See *VESA*.

VRAM, 13
Same thing as *video memory*.

W4W
A corny way to abbreviate Windows for Workgroups. See *WFW*.

wait state, 63
The time that a computer must wait — literally hang around — for its memory to catch up. A computer with zero wait states will be faster than one with wait states.

warranty, 122-123
An offer to repair or replace defective equipment where you pay only the labor costs. Most computers come with a 30-, 60-, or 90-day warranty. This is really all you need; extra money spent on extended warranty or service contracts is typically a waste of money. Refer to Chapter 13.

WFW
An abbreviation for the Windows for Workgroups operating system, which is a special networked version of Windows.

Windows, 22-23
An operating system designed to replace DOS as the PC's main operating system. Most new PCs will come with both DOS and Windows.

word processor, 33-34
Software that allows text to be composed, edited, and printed; it's the ultimate form of a typewriter. (Some computers are dedicated word processors — meaning that's all they do. Avoid them.)

write protect
A mechanism used to prevent the accidental writing to, erasing, or overwriting of data on disk. $5^1/_4$-inch diskettes use metallic tabs, $3^1/_2$-inch disks use a sliding tile. Very few hard disks offer any form of write protection.

WYSIWYG, 35
Pronounced "wizzy-wig," it stands for "What You See Is What You Get." WYSIWYG refers to a type of computer program that displays text or graphics (or both) on-screen exactly as they appear when printed.

XGA, 76

A graphics standard introduced by IBM to supplant its VGA graphics standard. XGA stands for eXtended Graphics Array, and it's pronounced ecks-jee-ay.

ZIF

An acronym standing for Zero Insertion Force. This type of socket makes it easy to install a microprocessor upgrade into your PC.

Symbols
$CALL, 153
286 (80286), 50
386 (80386), 49–50
386DX, 50
386SX, 50
486 (80486), 49–50
586 (80586), 49–50
65C816, 49
68020, 49
6908, 49
8514/a, 76

A
access time, 67, 115
AdLib sound card, 115
ads, buying a computer, 132–133
America Online, 38
Analog-to-Digital (A-to-D) port, 86, 89

B
BASIC programming language, 41
Baud rate, 112
benchmark, 53
binary, 60
binary digit, 61
BIOS (Basic Input/Output System), 21
bit, 61
bit width, 50, 61
boat anchors, 17

book
   about, 2–3
   read before purchase, 3
BPS (bits per second), 111–112
bundled software, 44
burn-in test, 123
bus, 93–96
   local, 95–96
   types of, 94–96
buying a computer
   ad tricks, 134
   common mistakes made, 139
   do not leave a deposit, 132
   final steps, 138–140
   getting quotes, 135
   haggling over price, 135
   put information all together, 129–132
   reading ads, 132–133
   service/technical support, 133
   software, 136
   when received, 131
   where from, 134–137
   where to spend extra money, 131
byte, 59–60

C
C programming language, 41
C++ programming language, 41
cables, printer, 99
cache, 54–55

Glossary and Index

CAD (Computer Assisted Design), 37
CD-ROM drive, 114–116
   access time, 115
   controllers, 115
   data transfer rate, 115
   proprietary controller, 115
   speed ratings, 115
Centronics port, 86–87
communications software, 38
   on-line services, 38
compatibility, 18
compilers, 41
computer literate, 2
computer stores
   locally owned, 135–136
   mail-order brand names, 137–138
   mail-order pieces parts, 138
   megastores, 137
   national chains, 136
computer systems
   about, 141–146
   questions, 152–153
   setting up PC, 141–145
computers, 8
   books, 156
   break in period, 145
   buying, 129–140
   buying used, 9
   five step buying process, 5–12
   hardware requirement effects on purchase, 8–10
   magazines, 155–156
   memory limitations, 61–62
   operating system, 17–23
   potential, 15–16
   revolution myth, 1–2
   service/support effects on purchase, 10–11
   setting up, 141–146
   software base compatibility, 18–19
   software effects on purchase, 7–8
   speed ratings, 52–53
   technology effects on purchase, 11–12
   user groups, 156–157
   uses for, 6–7, 13–16
contextual help, 28
controllers, 69
   CD-ROM drive, 115
conventional memory, 62
cooling fan, microprocessor, 50
CPS (characters per second), 102
CPU, 47
cursor, 91

D

data transfer rate, 115
databases, 16, 36
demo software, 44
deposits, to buy computer, 132
desktop PC, 11
desktop publishing, 35
Dhrystones microprocessor speed rating, 53
discount price, 135
disk drives, 65–73
   floppy, 70–73
   hard drive, 66–70
   permanent storage, 65
   questions, 149
diskettes, formatting, 72–73
DOS, operating system, 22–23
dot matrix printers, 100–103
   9-pin versus 24-pin, 101
   carriage width, 102
   CPS (characters per second), 102
   friction feed, 102–103
   NLQ (near letter quality), 101
   pin-feed, 103
   tractor-feed, 103
   true descenders, 101
dot pitch, 79
drawing programs, 37
drivers, printer, 106
drives, CD-ROM, 114–116

DS/DD, 72
DX, 50
DX2, 50–51
DX3, 52

E

ECP/EPP port, 86–87
ED, 72
education software, 39
Epson printers, 106
ergonomic, 82
expanded memory, 62
expansion cards, 93
expansion slots, 93, 110
extended memory, 62

F

fax/modems, 113
fixed disk, 67
flash programmable BIOS, 152
floating point operations, 53
floppy drives, 70–73
    densities, 71–72
    formatting disks, 72–73
    sides, 71–72
    sizes, 70–71
formatted, 72
free software, 27, 42–44
frequency, 79

G

games, 39
general questions, 153–154
gigabytes, 68
glossary, 159–188
graphics adapter, 76
graphics cards
    labeling, 76
    selecting, 76–77
graphics controller, 76
graphics software, 37

H

H.D.D., 133
hard copy, 8, 97
hard disk, 67
hard disk drive, 66, 133
hard drive, 8, 66–70
    access time, 67–68
    controllers, 69–70
    cost considerations, 69
    ecording head, 66
    speed measurements, 67–68
    storage capacity, 68
hard file, 67
hardware, 8
hardware requirements
    effects on computer purchase, 8–10
    software box information, 29–31
Hayes compatible modem, 112–113
Hayes SmartCom software, 112
HD, 72
help features, 27
help, where to go, 154
Hewlett-Packard printers, 106
High Capacity disks, 72
High Density disks, 72
home-budgeting software, 36

I

IBM printers, 106
IDE (Integrated Drive Electronics), 69
information, where to find, 155–157
ink jet printers, 103–104
Inport, 86, 89
integrated software, 7, 44–45
interlacing, 79
Internet, 38

J

joystick port, 86, 89–90

K

K, 60
keyboard questions, 149–150

keyboards, 80–82
    101-key Enhanced, 81
    ergonomic, 82
    selecting, 81
kilobyte, 60

L

laptop computer, 11
laser printers, 104–105
    p.p.m. (pages per minute), 105
layout, 35
lifetime warranty, 124
local bus, 95
Logitech mouse, 92

M

M, 59, 133
Macintosh, operating system, 22–23
mail-order brand names, 137–138
mail-order pieces parts, 138
manuals, reading, 143
math coprocessors, 51–52
MB, 59, 133
megabytes, 60, 133
megahertz, 51
megastores, 137
memory manager, 62
memory (RAM), 8, 57–63, 133
    bit width, 61
    buying considerations, 62–63
    bytes, 59
    computer limitations, 61–62
    conventional, 62
    expanded, 62
    extended, 62
    measuring, 59–60
    reason for, 58
    software requirements, 60–61
    temporary storage, 65
    video, 77
    wait state, 63

MHz, 51
microprocessors, 17–18, 47–55
    16 bit versus 32 bit, 50–51
    cache, 54–55
    cooling fan, 50
    Dhrystones speed rating, 53
    effects on memory limitations, 54
    families, 49
    Norton SI speed rating, 53
    offspring, 49
    power measurements, 50–51
    questions, 148
    Sieve of Eratosthenes speed rating, 53
    speed/megahertz, 51–54
    typing, 48–50
    Whetstones speed rating, 53
    Winstones speed rating, 53
Microsoft mouse, 92
MIDI port, 90
mistakes, made by first time buyers, 139
MO (Magneto-Optical) drive, 117
modem port, 86, 88
modems, 38, 109–113
    AT commands, 112
    baud rate, 112
    connection speeds, 111–112
    fax, 113
    Hayes compatible, 112–113
    internal versus external, 110–111
monitors, 75–79
    dot pitch, 79
    frequency, 79
    graphics controller/ adapter, 76–77
    graphics resolution, 77
    interlacing, 79
    questions, 149–150
    selecting, 78–79
    size, 78
    video board, 76
    video memory, 77

mouse, 91–93
   Logitech, 92
   Microsoft-compatible, 92
   trackballs, 93
   types of, 93
mouse pointer, 91
mouse port, 86, 89
multimedia, 41–42, 114–116
   hardware requirements, 116
   speakers, 116
   upgrade kits, 114–115

N

non-interlaced (NI), 79
Norton SI microprocessor
   speed rating, 53

O

objects, 37
office suite software, 45
offspring, 49
on-line help, 28
on-line services, 38
open architecture, 93
operating system, 9, 17–23
   DOS, 22–23
   Macintosh, 22–23
   OS/2, 22–23
   selecting, 22–23
   software base
      compatibility, 18–19
   UNIX, 22–23
   user friendly, 19–21
   Windows, 22–23
optical drive, 117
OS/2, operating system, 22–23

P

p.p.m. (pages per minute), 105
painting programs, 37
paper, printer, 100
parallel port, 86–87
PC, setting up, 141–146
   breaking in, 145
   finding parts, 142
   learning your system, 146
   putting it together, 142–144
   reading the manuals, 143
   save the boxes, 142
   turning on/off, 144–145
   where to put, 144
PCI bus, 95
Pentium, 49–50
peripherals, 8, 73, 109–119
   MO drive, 117
   modems, 109–113
   multimedia, 114–116
   questions, 150–151
   removable hard drives, 117
   scanners, 118
   sound cards, 114–116
   tape backup systems, 117–118
   UPS (uninterruptible
      power supply) 118–119
   WORM drive, 117
pixels, 77
ports, 85–91, 143
   Analog-to-Digital
      (A-to-D), 85, 89
   Centronics, 86–87
   ECP/EPP, 86–87
   Inport, 86, 89
   joystick 86, 89–90
   MIDI, 90
   modem, 86, 88
   mouse, 86, 89
   parallel, 86–87
   printer, 86–87
   RS-232, 86, 88
   SCSI, 85–86, 90–91
   serial, 86–88
power bar, 118
power protector, 118, 142
power strips, 118, 142
printer port, 86
printers, 8, 97
   cabling, 99
   compatibility issues, 106
   daisy wheel, 98
   dot matrix, 98, 100–103
   drivers, 106
   Epson, 106

Hewlett-Packard, 106
　　　IBM, 106
　　　ink jet, 98, 103–104
　　　laser, 98, 104–105
　　　paper types, 100
　　　price considerations, 98–99
　　　questions, 150–151
　　　thermal, 98, 104
　　　types of, 97–100
　processor, 47
　Prodigy, 38
　programming language
　　　software, 40–41
　proprietary controllers
　　　(sound cards), 115
　public domain software, 27, 43

Q

　questions
　　　$CALL, 153
　　　answers, 147–154
　　　case colors, 153
　　　computer systems, 152–153
　　　disk drives, 149
　　　general, 153–154
　　　integrated software, 147
　　　keyboards, 149–150
　　　learn to program, 154
　　　microprocessors, 148
　　　monitors, 149–150
　　　networks, 152
　　　peripherals, 150–151
　　　printers, 150–151
　　　shared disks, 147
　　　used computers, 152
　　　version numbers, 147
　　　viruses, 147
　QuickBASIC programming
　　　language software, 41
　quotes, buying a computer,
　　　135

R

RAM, 47, 57, 133
recording head, 66
recreation software, 39

removable hard drives, 117
ROM (Read-Only Memory), 21
RS-232 port, 86, 88

S

scanners, 118
SCSI (Small Computer
　　System Interface), 69–70
SCSI port, 85–86, 90–91
serial ports, 86–88, 110
service contracts, 123–124
service/support, 121–128, 133
　　after the sale, 124–125
　　effects on computer
　　　purchase, 10–11
　　lifetime warranty, 124
　　locating, 121–125
　　service contracts, 123–124
　　software, 27–29
　　User Groups, 125
　　warranty considerations,
　　　122–123
　　worksheet, 125–127
shareware, 43
Sieve of Eratosthenes
　　microprocessors speed
　　　rating, 53
single density, 71
software, 15
　　bundled, 44
　　CAD (Computer Assisted
　　　Design), 37
　　communications, 38
　　contextual help, 28
　　databases, 36
　　demo programs, 44
　　descriptions, 30–32
　　desktop publishing, 35
　　education, 39
　　effects on computer
　　　purchase, 7–8
　　free, 42–44
　　graphics, 37
　　hardware requirements,
　　　30–31
　　Hayes SmartCom, 112

193

help features, 27
home-budgeting, 36
integrated versus stand-alone, 44–45
memory manager, 62
memory requirements, 60–61
multimedia, 41–42
office suites, 45
on-line help, 28
programming, 40–41
public domain, 43
questions, 147–148
QuickBASIC, 41
recreation, 39
shareware, 43
shopping tips, 25–32
spreadsheets, 34–35
technical support, 27–29
test-drive, 25–26
user-friendly, 26–27
utility program, 39–40
VisiCalc, 35
VisualBASIC, 41
word processors, 33–34
software base, 18
software box, system requirements, 29–31
sound card, 114
   AdLib, 115
   compatibility issues, 115
   SoundBlaster, 115
   speakers, 116
SoundBlaster sound card, 115
speakers, multimedia, 116
spreadsheets, 34–35
SS/DD, 71
SX, 50–51

T

tape backup systems, 117–118
telecom program, 38
terms, 159–188
testing computers, 145
text editors, 40
thermal printers, 104

trackballs, 93
tricks, to make price look cheap, 134

U

UNIX, operating system, 22–23
upgrade, 131
UPS (uninterruptible power supply), 118–119, 142
used computers, service/support issues, 9
User Groups, 125
user-hostile, 27
utility program, 39–40

V

VESA bus, 95
video board, 76
Video Memory, 144
Video RAM, 133
VisiCalc software, 35
VisualBASIC programming language software, 41
VRAM, 133

W

warranty, 122–123
   lifetime, 124
Whetstones microprocessor speed rating, 53
windowing, 35
Windows, operating system, 22–23
Winstones microprocessor speed rating, 53
word processors, 33–34
worksheet
   computer, 129–130
   dealer service/support, 125–127
WORM (Write Once, Read Many) drive, 117
WYSIWYG (What-You-See-Is-What-You-Get), 35

IDG BOOKS WORLDWIDE REGISTRATION CARD

RETURN THIS REGISTRATION CARD FOR FREE CATALOG

Title of this book: Buy That Computer! 1995 Edition

My overall rating of this book: ❏ Very good [1] ❏ Good [2] ❏ Satisfactory [3] ❏ Fair [4] ❏ Poor [5]

How I first heard about this book:
❏ Found in bookstore; name: [6] ❏ Book review: [7]
❏ Advertisement: [8] ❏ Catalog: [9]
❏ Word of mouth; heard about book from friend, co-worker, etc.: [10] ❏ Other: [11]

What I liked most about this book:

What I would change, add, delete, etc., in future editions of this book:

Other comments:

Number of computer books I purchase in a year: ❏ 1 [12] ❏ 2-5 [13] ❏ 6-10 [14] ❏ More than 10 [15]

I would characterize my computer skills as: ❏ Beginner [16] ❏ Intermediate [17] ❏ Advanced [18] ❏ Professional [19]

I use ❏ DOS [20] ❏ Windows [21] ❏ OS/2 [22] ❏ Unix [23] ❏ Macintosh [24] ❏ Other: [25] _____
(please specify)

I would be interested in new books on the following subjects:
(please check all that apply, and use the spaces provided to identify specific software)

❏ Word processing: [26] ❏ Spreadsheets: [27]
❏ Data bases: [28] ❏ Desktop publishing: [29]
❏ File Utilities: [30] ❏ Money management: [31]
❏ Networking: [32] ❏ Programming languages: [33]
❏ Other: [34]

I use a PC at (please check all that apply): ❏ home [35] ❏ work [36] ❏ school [37]
❏ other: [38] _____

The disks I prefer to use are ❏ 5.25 [39] ❏ 3.5 [40] ❏ other: [41] _____

I have a CD ROM: ❏ yes [42] ❏ no [43]

I plan to buy or upgrade computer hardware this year: ❏ yes [44] ❏ no [45]

I plan to buy or upgrade computer software this year: ❏ yes [46] ❏ no [47]

Name: _____ Business title: [48] _____
Type of Business: [49]
Address (❏ home [50] ❏ work [51]/Company name: _____)
Street/Suite#
City [52]/State [53]/Zipcode [54]: Country [55]

❏ **I liked this book!**
You may quote me by name in future IDG Books Worldwide promotional materials.

My daytime phone number is _____

IDG BOOKS

THE WORLD OF COMPUTER KNOWLEDGE

❏ **YES!**
Please keep me informed about IDG's World of Computer Knowledge. Send me the latest IDG Books catalog.

BUSINESS REPLY MAIL
FIRST CLASS MAIL   PERMIT NO. 2605   FOSTER CITY, CALIFORNIA

IDG Books Worldwide
919 E Hillsdale Blvd, STE 400
Foster City, CA 94404-9691

NO POSTAGE
NECESSARY
IF MAILED
IN THE
UNITED STATES